Love & Art™

A Story of Love, Deception and Hope

By 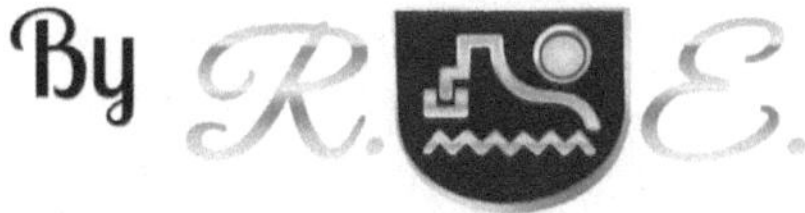

Love and Art

Printed in the United States of America

This book is dedicated to all of my ancestors resting in Paradise and my friends who left to early: grandfathers, grandmothers, my mother and father, aunts, uncles, siblings, Kim Ealy Daniels and Dr. Eve Allen, and cousins.

And to those who exist: family members, friends, Wayne Wilson, Dr. Ahmses Maat, and many more… thank you for being instrumental in my life and for all your support.

Okay, and yes… you too, LaRhonda Angelisa. Thank you for inspiring me to express your artistic creativity.
Love you, girl.

Xenophobia is a word of fear of others. If we continue to be in fear of one another, we will not be able to continue to exist on planet earth.

This book has been written to feed the human spirit, and based upon the individual, it has the potential to make you into a better person, wife, husband, daughter, son, and human being.

If you doubt anything you don't understand, you can fact-check it and find it true. So, read it with an open mind and never be afraid to look at things from a different perspective; it will take your thought process places where you would never imagine ever going.

CHAPTER **ONE**

The dimly lit nightclub was packed, and with the band loudly playing the current chart toppers, the dance floor is no less so. Andre walked through the crowded room, smoothly making his way to the bar.

A handsome man in his thirties, standing at least 6 feet and 5 inches, with dark chocolate skin, Andre is dressed well: blue pinstripe suit, tilted brim, and Stacey Adams. He is looking to flirt with whoever he can. Finding a seat, he watches for a moment. Lifting his incognito shades, he reveals his beautiful dark brown eyes. Then, slightly lowering one brow, looking like a boss player, he quickly spots what he is looking for from across the room. He turns to the bartender and orders a drink.

"Let me get an Apple Martini, and could you send a bottle of Cristal to that table full of beautiful women over there?"

The bartender smiled. "Alright, I ain't mad at ya, playa. That'll be $85.95."

Andre paid his bill, making sure to add a tip, and then he picked up his drink and strutted to the table where three women sat. "Ladies, what's going on?" he said confidently.

The woman sitting opposite him looked up and responded first. "Ahhh, we doing fine, sugar... and so are you."

"Girl, you ain't never lied. This Negro is fine," the woman to her right remarked.

The third woman set her drink down and looked Andre up and down. "Ya'll need to quit trippin' over this man. He ain't all that; he probably got a wife and kids at home."

"Girl, this negro can have a wife, a mistress, a concubine, and fifteen bad snotty nose kids scattered across town!" the first woman replied. "I don't give a damn… Boy, you just keep sending that Cristal to a sister."

Her unimpressed friend smirked knowingly. "Well, since you put it like that," she scoffed, lifting her drink back to her lips where her lipstick had already smeared.

As the music changed to a slow romantic rhythm, Andre gently held his hand out to the woman who hadn't yet fallen for his charms. "Come dance with me, baby."

Catching a quick glimpse of Andre's left ring finger, she noticed it was bare, so smiling, she looked up at the well-dressed man before her as if he was a prince coming to sow his royal oats. "Well, okay, I guess..." she said, rising, a bit tipsy, from her chair.

As she and Andre began moving toward the crowded dance floor, one of the women shouted for her to *show that negro what you workin' with!* while the second laughed in agreement, "With your intoxicated behind."

Andre led his unstable partner to the center of the dance floor that squeaked underneath their feet and then pulled her close to him. As they slowly found each other's unfamiliar and uncoordinated rhythm, they finally began to step together, taking advantage of the dance to get to know one another.

"I'm Andre... tell me, baby, what's your name?" Andre asked.

"I'm Lucille. I'm a Gemini... and no, I ain't got no man, and I ain't been with no man in five looong years. But I do need a man, starting right now."

"Damn, baby, how much longer can you go without a man like that?"

Lucille tucked her sweaty head into Andre's buffed chest and inhaled his expensive cologne. He always chose the highest quality ingredients with a rich-smelling scent. The aroma was no match for a lonely stretch of celibacy. Grabbing him like a teddy bear, she said, "I'm going to tell you honestly, honey, I have so many sleepless nights and don't really think I can go another one without someone to hold."

Andre couldn't believe his ears; there was a desperate

cry in her voice that was vulnerable and apparently in need.

As her heart fluttered rapidly, Lucille gravitated even closer toward him; her knees weakening as if she would collapse. In that moment, Andre knew he had captured her in a lustrous web. His only thought was *I'm getting laid tonight!* He didn't want to waste any time, and his excitement certainly wouldn't let him wait.

"Baby, come on and go with me. Come on over to my place," he whispered into her ear, words stolen straight from Teddy Pendergrass's hit "Come Go with Me." All along in his mind, he knew his place was a hotel.

Lucille was too sexually bothered to even notice. "I thought you would never ask," she whispered back.

Andre smoothly walked a slightly staggering Lucille off the dance floor, heading directly for the exit door. Lucille's friends, Pam and Nicole, were still at the table with their drinks and watched the two of them leaving, mouths agape. They couldn't believe their eyes.

"Girl, do you see what I'm seeing?" Pam asked incredulously.

Nicole nodded her head. "Yeah, Girl. What is she thinking? She just met him!"

Neither of the women could believe what they'd just witnessed. Still, since there wasn't much they could do about it, Pam simply shook her head in disbelief, Nicole took another sip of the champagne Andre had bought them, and they both resumed their conversation until a Lenny Williams song, "Cause I Love You," came on.

"Girl, that's my jam!" Nicole excitedly shouted.

"Mine too," Pam exclaimed as the pair slowly bobbed their heads and sang along to the music playing in the background.

At around eight the next morning, Andre was awakened by the sun creeping through the window and passing over his face. As he came around, he realized where he was and quickly jumped up, frantically racing around the room, trying to separate his clothes from hers and get them on before waking her up.

It hadn't worked. His furtive movements only served to wake Lucille, and as she sat upright in the king-sized bed, she was in utter astonishment — still in a sleepy haze, trying to piece together where she was and what had happened the night before. All she was sure of was that she had a splitting headache from drinking too much and that an incredibly handsome man was in the room with her, currently racing to get away.

"Is everything alright? What's wrong?" She asked, rubbing her eyes and smoothing down her hair, still slightly messed up from her night's sleep.

"Oh, uhhh... yeah, baby. I'm just late for work, and I have to hurry before I get fired for being late again."

Confused, Lucille didn't know what to do or think. She had just slept with a total stranger; she knew nothing about him. "Wait a minute, is your name B.B. King? Because I'm starting to feel like I've just been played."

Andre quickly tucked his fully buttoned shirt into his pant leg and smiled. *Don't hate the playa', hate the game,* he thought to himself as he slowly turned to Lucille, grabbed her hand, and kissed it. Calmly, he responded, "Ahh, baby, I can't believe you've forgotten my name already! It's Andre... and naw, you got it all wrong. I would never, ever, ever, ever play a woman as beautiful as yourself!"

His soothing low voice made Lucille grin from ear to ear, and she felt more at ease. Perhaps she hadn't made such a huge mistake sleeping with him after all. "Will I see you later?" she asked with a sense of confidence. "Because I was looking forward to you meeting my children."

The spontaneity of Andre's actions had caught up with him; "Your children?" he playfully caterwauled, grabbing his car keys from the nightstand. "Sure, baby. I love kids. Just write your number down for me, and I'll call you later."

Lucille reached over the side of the bed to pick up her evening clutch, pulled out her business card, and handed it to Andre, which he slipped into his suit coat pocket before giving her a kiss on the forehead and moving toward the door. On his way out, he made sure, once again, to promise her that he would call her later.

Lucille continued to sit up in the bed, still in utter amazement and unsure of exactly what had just happened. Before she knew it, Andre had shut the door, and she was alone.

CHAPTER TWO

Andre cautiously made his way from the city to a beautiful, two-story, three-car garage house in the suburbs, complete with a stunning garden and immaculate finishes.

He hesitated for a moment at the front door — his typically calm and collected nature becoming worried and flustered. Nevertheless, Andre attempted to get his composure together, pulling a handkerchief out of his pocket to wipe his brow. Slowly, he stuck the key into the lock, and then, after taking a breath or two, turned the doorknob.

Andre crept down the hallway, being extremely careful not to make a sound, and prepared to head up the stairs, but before he could do so, he was surprisingly greeted by his wife, Monica, who seemed to appear out of nowhere.

"Good morning, babe. Did you eat yet? Are you hungry?" She asked with a gentle yet peculiar smile.

As always, he was struck by her natural beauty and lovely nature; she hadn't even asked him where he'd been. But at this moment, Andre was eager to get upstairs to put his wedding band back on his finger. "That sounds great, baby," he said with deceptive ease, not quite matching his erratic behavior, all while keeping his left hand slightly behind his back. "I'm famished! Let me jump in the shower, and I'll be right down," he continued, kissing her on the lips and quickly running up the stairs to avoid her noticing anything missing.

As Andre rushed up the stairs, the inept handling of his step forced him to stumble. Catching himself, he regained his balance and headed to the main bedroom, trying to remember which suit jacket he had hidden the ring in this time, but he couldn't locate it in any of them. Discombobulated, he headed into the bathroom to take a shower. Turning on the water and hopping in, Andre momentarily managed to forget his careless ways as he cleaned himself. Once he had dried off, he stepped back into the bedroom —he needed to find that ring.

Upon entering the room, Andre noticed that his clothes had been neatly ironed and laid out on the bed for him. *Who's the man,* he thought to himself. *I'm the man.* He was no longer distracted by the fear of getting caught cheating, contemplating that she might not notice that he wasn't wearing his ring. Unable to resist the aroma wafting from downstairs, Andre hurried to get dressed, telling himself that he would continue the hunt later, he followed the delicious smell to the kitchen, where Monica was hovering over the stainless-steel stove that she somehow kept spotless even while cooking, finishing up the meal she had made just for him.

"Baby, what is that you've got smelling so good up in here?"

"Oh, Baby, I fixed all of your favorites. I made you some eggs, hash browns, grits, and wheat biscuits. You have a seat, and I'll fix you a plate."

With an ego bigger than his usual appetite, he was eager to gulp down his food so he could hurriedly get to work. Andre took a seat at the kitchen table without the slightest idea of what lay before him. He suddenly noticed a stack of credit card bills and phone numbers that he had in his jacket pocket, and... there it was. His wedding band was sitting on top of the pile, all neatly placed in front of him. He began to stutter, trying to make any coherent word come out of his mouth. "Baby, what... what's all of this?"

Monica remained composed. "Well, Andre, I was hoping you could tell me," she replied, slowly cracking her neck from one side to the other. "What *is* all of this?"

At a loss for words, Andre had no idea what to say — he was simply caught. He couldn't snap his way out even if his life depended on it.

Before he could bring himself to say a thing, Monica's calm, sweet voice filled the silence. "Oh, that's okay. I can tell by the phone numbers and receipts I found in your pockets that Susan, Latasha, Jackie, and Robin are all wearing brand-new Victoria's Secret lingerie over at the Ambassador Inn, where you seem to be quite frequently.

Shocked, Andre blurted out, "Oh, no, Monica. It's not what you think!"

"You know what, Andre? You're probably right... I'm probably imagining that extra $1000 charge on my American Express bill. I'm sure my imagination is getting the best of me. I know you love me and would never do anything to hurt me... right?"

"That's right, baby. You know I love you, I -"

Cutting him short, straight, and to the point, her voice not quite as sweet as it had been earlier, Monica retorted, "After ten years, you still don't know what love is. I just hope you were smart enough to use protection at least once. Did you think about saving money for your daughter's birthday gift? You haven't forgotten that we're celebrating her ninth birthday this Saturday, have you? On her way to school this morning, she mentioned that you promised her a pony. We don't even have room for a pony, Andre."

"Can we talk about this later?"

"No, let's talk about this now!"

Andre wanted to be anywhere but here, so he glanced at his watch." Oh, shoot, look at the time. I've got to get to work; I'm already running late Monica. We'll talk later, okay?"

"Whatever, Andre. You have a nice day," she said sarcastically.

Andre tried to give his wife another kiss on the mouth,

but this time, she intentionally turned her head so that he only got her cheek. Monica quickly wiped his kiss off with the back of her hand as if she had just been smeared with filth. Sighing, he turned around and left her standing amongst the breakfast dishes and the pile of proof on the kitchen table.

CHAPTER **THREE**

The day of the anticipated birthday party for Andre and Monica's daughter, Vicky, arrived. It was sunny and bright, with no clouds and a small crowd of children and a few adults gathered in the beautifully decorated backyard fit for a princess.

Monica always went out of her way to be the perfect mother. This day would not go unnoticed as well. Fearing she would receive little or no help from Andre, she managed to stash away extra cash so Vicky would not be disappointed. Somehow, she felt content in doing so, even if she was way over the original budget.

Everyone outside was singing and dancing to the music on the radio. It was a joyous day, with beautiful smiles on everyone's faces and laughter in the air. Vicky was jumping rope with her friends, delighted to have a day that was all about her.

In the kitchen, Monica chatted with some of her

longtime friends and co-worker while keeping an eye on the kids. They helped her prepare party food as they talked about work and life.

Inevitably, Monica's friend, Channelle, anxiously asked the question hanging in the air. "Monica, where's Andre?"

Monica had her excuse already prepared. "Oh, he had to work today, but he should be home shortly," she said, casually putting chips into colorful bowls.

Her friend, Terry, chimed in playfully. "Hmm, yeah, he's at work, alright!"

Monica had known it was coming and decided to play it off. "Naw, it's not like that. My man loves me."

Another of her closest friends, Michelle, walked inside from where she had been standing in the yard, overhearing the conversation, and joined in. "Monica, I'm sure your man does love you, but girl, you don't have to play make-believe with us. We know what's going on."

"Girl… what are you talking about, Michelle?" Monica fired back a little too quickly.

"Girl, please... you know exactly what she's talking about," Terry retorted.

Michelle looked Monica right in the eye. "Look, Monica. We've been friends since grade school, and if we didn't care about you, we wouldn't say a thing. But the truth is... yes, your man probably does love you, but unfortunately, he's constantly been seen around town loving about four or five other hoochies-"

Channelle cut her off before she could say anything more. "Wait a minute, Michelle. Do you hear what you're saying? Those are some strong accusations you two are making. What proof do you have?"

Monica sighed and looked at her friends. "Okay, okay, stop… everybody, just stop! You're right. I can't do this anymore. I've been trying to keep everything together, but uh-uh. You don't need any proof; trust me, it has all been substantiated. Everything you're saying is true. I've known what this low-down dirty, cheating negro has been doing for years. I thought that if I were the perfect mother and wife, one day, Andre would want to be the perfect husband."

Channelle touched Monica's arm in sympathy. "Girl, you are the perfect mother and wife. You have been tap-dancing around this fool for years, and you deserve better for you and your daughter. You have to communicate and let this man know exactly how you feel and what it is you want out of life. Life is too short and too precious — not to mention unpredictable."

"You know she's right," Michelle added. "You've got to communicate to make a marriage work. Have you considered counseling?"

Monica shook her head. "That's just it... I don't even want to make this treacherous marriage work anymore. I want out. I can no longer pretend that everything is storybook wonderful. It's been months since Andre and I have even slept in the same bed because I'm afraid he might bring home something that might kill me five years from now."

"Girl, you know what they say, if it ain't broke, don't

fix it. Well, when you know it's broke, fix him," Terry commented, rubbing Monica's shoulder.

"That's right," Michelle agreed. "Get him fixed like they do dogs. Castrate his black behind, and then you won't have to worry about that negro bringing you home nothing."

Channelle took a slow, deep breath and spoke in a more sympathetic tone. "Monica, I'm so sorry. I know exactly how you feel. I went through the same mess with my first husband, and as women, we just want to give up on men altogether. And yes, the first thing we say is, "all men are dogs," but the fact is, there are a hell of a lot of dogs out there wagging their tails because they have not yet grasped the basic concepts of commitment, responsibility, or accountability. But at the same time, there are a few good men still out there as well."

Although furious, Monica was relieved to have confided in what she feared most, the truth — finally, a chance to share with her dearest friends, confirming what she had known all along. Turning away from them, she walked over to the kitchen drawer, opened it, pulled out the local directory, sat down at the wooden round table, and slowly flipped to the attorney section. While tears of relief began to roll down her face, Monica circled a name before sighing as if she was almost gasping for air, realizing that despite denials and previous accusations, there would be no reprieve for Andre; he would no longer be able to thwart her from accomplishing the actions needed to break free from a deceitful marriage.

Her friends watched her movements and came over to hug and console her once they recognized what she had done. Channelle wiped her tears, and Michelle and Terry let her know how proud they were of her, dancing with glee — at least until Monica shot them a frustrated look. Instantly, they stop and grow silent. As soon as Monica dropped her gaze, the two women gave each other a "high five."

Outside, Vicky and her friends were jumping double-dutch, laughing and shrieking. While Vicky jumped, two of her friends twirled the rope and sang.

Miss Mary Mack Mack Mack,
all dressed in black black black…

"Vicky, where yo daddy at?" one friend, Jazmine, asked, keeping time with the rope.

"He'll be here! He's at work right now. He always works late."

"My daddy works a lot, too," Nigel exclaimed. "He ain't never home."

"My dad and I are tight! We do everything together," exclaimed Chris, the youngest in the group. "We even dress alike sometimes!"

This comment was followed up by Elizabeth, the other

friend spinning the rope. "My daddy says I'm a princess! He gives me everything I want."

Jazmine says her father does, too; he calls her the prettiest girl in the world — besides her mommy.

Jawon, the last in the group of children to speak, piped up: "Yo mom ain't pretty! At least not as pretty as all of my moms!"

Everyone paused to look at Jawon, confused. One of them asked, "*All* of your moms?"

"Yeah, my dad's a pimp. I got a new mom every day of the week!"

Chris laughed. "Man, yo daddy ain't no pimp. Quit playing."

"What's a pimp?" Vicky asked.

"A pimp is somebody that drives a big pink car, walks with a limp, wears big hats, and dresses really sharp," explained Nigel, matter-of-factly.

Chris smirked. "Vicky, a pimp is someone who takes advantage of a woman. He's not a nice person. My mom told me she would beat my behind if I ever tried to be one."

"Ya don't know nothing," Jawon interjected. "My daddy is super cool, and all the women love him. When I grow up, I'm gonna be just like him."

"Yeah... broke and lonely," replied Jazmine, causing all the kids to laugh and fall out.

Just then, Monica opened the back door. "Hey, ya'll! Time to come and sing happy birthday and have some cake and ice cream."

The kids shouted joyfully and ran inside for food, starving after their play. They took turns washing their hands in the restroom and then piled into the dining room for a selection of pizza, hot dogs, and snacks Monica had laid out. Chris reached for a slice only to have his hand popped by Channelle, his mother, before he could grab anything.

"Hold up, young man," she scolded. "I know I've taught you better than that! Everyone, bow your head so that we can bless this food."

They all did as instructed, and Channelle lead them in prayer:

> Dear Lord, as we gather here today, we want to thank you for providing us with roofs over our heads and nourishment for our bodies. Lord, please bless us all as we stand before you on this joyous occasion to celebrate the birth of one of your precious angels; she is one of the most deserving and wonderful gifts you could have given us... so Lord, today, as we celebrate her and shower her with gifts, we give you all the praise as we say thank you, Lord... and Amen.

The combined voices of adults and children echoed her "Amen," and the kids immediately began piling food onto their plates and stuffing their faces.

"Wow! Thank you, Channelle. That was beautiful. I wish I could pray like that," Monica exclaimed, watching the kids fill themselves with goodies.

"Girl, there's nothing to it. It's in your heart... all you do is transfer it to your mouth and share your thoughts and words with God. You really should come to church with me sometime."

"You know what, I would like that. I think me and Vicky will come. Let me know the next time you're going."

"Well, I'm in church every Sunday morning, so I'll be calling you tomorrow morning since tomorrow is Sunday," Channelle said, smiling.

Monica smiled back and then discreetly went into the kitchen to get the cake for Vicky. She lit the candles and walked back into the dining room as Channelle turned off the lights. The group sang "Happy Birthday" to Vicky, with the kids yelling and jumping for joy as they did so.

"Okay, Vicky… make a wish and blow out your candles!" Monica ordered.

Vicky closed her eyes, made her wish... and then hesitated. Opening her eyes long enough to take a quick look at the front door, she drew in a deep breath and blew her candles out as hard as possible.

CHAPTER **FOUR**

It was now 1:00 am, and as usual, Andre was sneaking into the house as if he were an irresponsible teenager needing to avoid punishment. He carefully placed a large gift wrapped with a beautiful bright pink ribbon tied into a bow onto the living room table and then headed for the stairs. But he didn't make it that far; he was stopped dead in his tracks by Monica, who had fallen asleep on the living room sofa while awaiting his arrival.

"Do you know what time it is?" she said, furious, somehow managing to keep her voice low, trying hard not to wake up Vicky. "Where have you been this time?!"

Shocked that she was waiting up for him, Andre stuttered, trying to explain. "I had to finish up a few things at the office. How did everything go? Did Vicky have fun? I'm so sorry that I missed everything."

"Sorry?" she responded incredulously. "You don't have to apologize to me… unfortunately, I already know what to expect from you by now. But why do you have to let Vicky down? It was her birthday, Andre, and you come stepping up in here late as usual. And don't act like I'm some stupid, naïve fool that don't know what you've been up to. I've been putting up with your lying, cheating, and deceiving ways for years."

"Hold up! Hell naw... don't even come at me like that, woman! I've been working hard to keep a roof over your damn head, and you gon' come at me like I'm somebody's child."

"Funny you should say that because that's how you're acting!"

As their argument continued, Vicky woke up. Hearing the shouting from downstairs, she got out of bed and opened her bedroom door to see what was happening. She knew to be quiet, so she hung out on the upstairs landing to hear what her parents were saying.

"Look, like Fanny Lou Hamer, I'm sick and tired of being sick and tired, and I'm through… I'm done! We're done… It's over, Andre! I should have done this a long time ago," Monica exclaimed.

"You know what? You're right! This has gone on long enough, so why don't you do us both a favor and get out of my face, woman? I'm tired, too. Sleepy from staying out all night."

Monica couldn't quite believe what she was hearing. "Negro, please…" she shouted, slapping him across the face in sheer rage at his audacity to say such a thing to her.

Andre, shocked, responded, "Woman! Are you crazy or

something? Baby, don't do that. I'm not trying to go to jail tonight!"

Monica knew this would be the final straw for her and spoke more quietly now. "Well, if you don't want to go to jail, then just go to hell, Andre. Get out of my face," she said, exhausted.

Andre was stunned. How could his wife of ten years speak to him in such a way — act in such a way? In the entire decade of their marriage, she had never so much as raised her voice at him, and now this? "Is this really what you want? You think you can do this without me? Take it, take it all, Monica. I'll grab my things and get up out of your life."

"That's just it... you haven't been in my life for quite a long time now. Your shit is all packed up in a box to the left," Monica replied as she pointed toward the corner of the living room.

Andre followed the direction of her finger and saw his clothes and personal belongings had been thrown into a huge pile. He could only stare at his wife in disbelief.

Monica was doing everything she could to remain as strong as possible, but she could no longer hold the tears back. She was tired of fighting. Sitting back on the couch, she began to weep, crying out ten years' worth of tears.

Still angry and unfazed, Andre walked past her, grabbed a few of his things from the pile, and walked out the door.

When Vicky heard the door slam behind her father, she came out from her spot on the landing and ran down the stairs to hug her mom. With tears rolling down her own cheeks, she begged her mother to stop crying. "Daddy's going to come back, Mommy. Please stop crying... Daddy's going to come back," Vicky cried out, again and again, wrapping herself around her mom.

The two of them hold one another, wiping each other's tears.

~

Vicky awoke the following morning, still on the sofa, holding onto her mother. The first thing she saw in the light beaming through the front window was the large gift box sitting on the table in front of her. Sitting up, she took the card from the top of the gift and read it to herself:

Happy Birthday, Vicky!
From your father, with love.

Unable to contain her excitement, Vicky woke her mom, begging her to let her open the gift.

Monica slowly stretched, wiping her eyes. "Wow! Well, of course, baby. Go ahead... let's see what it is."

Vicky impatiently ripped the paper off, then quickly opened the box. "Ooo, Mommy, look! Daddy got me these pretty colored pencils and paints. And charcoal, and paper, and crayons, and all these paint brushes, too," Vicky said, speaking at double speed with excitement.

"Wow, you've got your own little art studio there,"

Monica replied. She was still half asleep but smiling to see her daughter's happiness.

"Yep, and I like it, mommy. I'm going to draw a beautiful picture for you and Daddy!"

"Okay, baby. But before you do, why don't you go get cleaned up first while I fix us some breakfast."

"Okay, Mommy. I'm going to take a bath, get dressed, come eat, and then I'm going to draw and paint all day long!" Vicky said, already on her feet and running towards the bathroom.

Just as Monica was headed to the kitchen to make breakfast for the two of them, the phone rang. It was Channelle calling to invite her and Vicky to church that morning.

"Hey, I almost forgot today is Sunday. But sure, we would love to go," Monica answered, cradling the phone between her ear and shoulder as she began cooking.

"Great! Trust me... you guys will enjoy yourselves. You ought to drag Andre along with you."

"Oh, girl, we really fell out last night. I don't think he's coming back anytime soon."

"I'm so sorry to hear that. Just pray about it; God will make a way."

Monica sighed. "Actually, it's okay. I feel like the weight of the whole world has been lifted from my shoulders. The chains around my heart have been removed, and now I'm going to live my life for me and my daughter. She needs me more than ever right now."

"Well, as long as you're good, I'm happy for you.

Service starts at 10, so I'll be over about 9:30 to pick you two up."

Monica confirmed that she and Vicky would be ready and then hung up the phone. She hurried to finish breakfast as Vicky came down the stairs and into the kitchen. "Vicky, Ms. Channelle just called to invite us to church, so when you finish your breakfast, you run back upstairs and put on a cute dress for church, okay?"

"Okay, Mommy. But when we come back from church, I get to draw and paint, right?"

"Of course, baby. You can draw and paint when we get back until your little heart is content."

Monica looked at her beautiful little girl. For the first time in a long time, she felt as if everything would be okay after all.

Andre sat in his one-bedroom apartment, unsure of what to do with himself. All he had done since leaving was reflect on what a wonderful life he once had with his wife and daughter. Unfortunately, now it had all fallen apart. He looked at the divorce papers in his hand and picked up the phone to call Monica. She was the epitome of God-fearing — short in stature with an even dark-brown complexion and loved wearing a natural curly afro with big hoop earrings that were always clip-on. She never believed in piercings.

As the tears run from Andre's eyes, his voice is much

softer than his usual loud manly voice when he's trying to get his point across. The irritation in his language is muttered when she picks up. "Hello, beautiful."

"What do you want this time?"

"I want you, baby… repeating himself but this time stumbling, I- I- I want you. I'm trying to imagine life without you and my daughter, and I can't. I didn't realize how much I loved you. My heart aches for you every night."

"Well… You should have thought about that beforehand, Andre!" Vicky shouted. She loved saying his name when he messed up; it made her feel better. "Love should have brought you home."

"Are you sure you want to go through with this?" He begged, desperate for her to give in to him.

"Positive," She replied flatly, yet resolute.

Andre fell quiet as he attempted to hold back his anger. For years he had been able to stand trial inside his home, but today Vicky's gavel hit hard. She was the prosecutor, jury, and judge. Andre was what society considered to be a conscious brother, based on his ancestral knowledge and awareness of a strong black man surviving and providing for his family in America. Maybe Monica was right after all. He once overheard her telling one of her friends on the phone that until he recognized the sacred vows of marriage and what commitment really stood for, he was nothing more than an educated fool. The thought of losing his family was unbearable, but he knew letting his anger out would get him nowhere.

"Are you there?" Monica's voice brought him back to the present moment.

"Yes, Monica, I'm here."

"Is there anything else you have to say before I hang up this phone?"

Trying not to let his emotions get the best of him, with watery eyes, Andre replied, "No, I'm going to give you what you want."

Monica raised her voice a notch. "You're not giving me what I want, Andre. You're giving me what I need. I don't even want alimony; all I need is child support for my daughter. I'll see you in court."

Monica hung up the phone, and Andre slammed his fist down on the coffee table in front of him and threw his phone across the room. It hit the wall and clattered to the floor. Out of anger, he shouted "ungrateful winch," expecting this outlet for his rage to make him feel better somehow, but all he felt was empty and alone.

CHAPTER **FIVE**

As Vicky sat in her school counselor's office, she tried to recall the first time she ever painted something. Thinking back to how art had been there for her throughout her childhood gave her confidence. All too often, when mundane tendencies try to overshadow her gifted artistic abilities and when she is unsure about the future, she reflects on the gift her father had given her on her ninth birthday. It was a blur, but also a sense of relief that even he had believed in her once.

In the ten years since the divorce of her parents, Vicky had leaned on art as a means of coping with the normalcy of life, which is what had brought her to Mrs. Carter's office today — it was time to start thinking about college and all she could dream about was an art scholarship.

"Vicky, I've been hearing nothing but great things about you," Mrs. Carter said, snapping her out of her daydream. "You have managed to maintain a 3.9 grade-point average in all of your classes, and it has been brought to my attention that you are an exceptionally talented artist. Your art teacher, Mr. Ashworth, informed us that you are the most promising out of all his students.

Vicky's smile was so big that the gap in her teeth was quite visible.

"Remember the extra assignments he gave you to complete during Christmas break? It was more like a secret challenge, and he said you passed with flying colors. No pun intended," Mrs. Carter continued. "I hope you know that with your GPA, art skills, and top SAT scores, there is a very strong possibility that we can get you a full-ride scholarship to practically any school of your choice."

Vicky couldn't quite believe what she was hearing; this was amazing news. However, she didn't allow herself to get too excited. Understanding that Mrs. Carter was only there to offer academic solutions such as college applications, Vicky thanked her for her time and excused herself. However, the thrill of attending college was short-lived, as she felt more confused than before the meeting.

Walking down the hall, Vicky passed other students, her mind in a daze. Her shoulder bumped into every other lock hanging from the lockers, not realizing that her equilibrium was off, wondering whether she really could go to college or not. Then, as she walked out of the school, she saw Chris waiting for her so they could walk home together.

"Vicky! Hey, there you are... do you know I've been

looking for you everywhere? I had asked everyone where you been," he called out as he came toward her.

Chris was a young man with a slender build and a nice fade. Always dressed to impress the ladies, he rocked Nikes like nobody's business. He also loved wearing Polo shirts, his Levi jeans were pressed with an impeccable crease straight down the middle, and his style was highly coordinated to catch every young lady's attention. But he only had eyes for one, Vicky. Since junior high, the two of them had been walking back and forth to and from school, but Chris had carried a crush on Vicky since they were kids. He just never knew how to bridge the gap from "good friend" to boyfriend.

"Sorry, Chris. I had to talk to Mrs. Carter. She was telling me I have an opportunity to utilize my artistic skills to go to college on a full ride."

"Woah, that's amazing, Vicky. What school are you going to go to?" he asked, genuinely impressed.

"Chris, that's just it. I don't think I'm going to go to college just yet," she replied, unable to hide the disappointment in her voice.

Chris cuts in immediately, "Why? What's the problem? Getting a scholarship and going to college is a great opportunity. I think you should at least give it some more thought. What about your mom? What does she think?"

"She doesn't know yet, and I'm not quite sure how to tell her. I know that she has been struggling ever since my dad left us, so I really feel as though I need to stay home to help her out."

Chris didn't quite understand where Vicky was coming from but offered his opinion. "Well, I'm sure she would be very proud to know you have such a wonderful opportunity, and at the same time, I know she's going to be highly disappointed if you didn't let her know, and then she finds out from someone else."

By this time, the pair had arrived outside Vicky's house, and she had come to a conclusion. "Chris, you know you're right. I have to at least let my mom know that I have a chance to go to college; that will make her very happy and very proud of me too. However, I've made up my mind... I'm not going to college right away. I want to make sure my mom's okay, so I'm going to get a job and help my mom out as soon as possible."

Still a little bewildered, Chris looked at her with a sympathetic smile and nodded his head anyway. "Okay, Vicky, I can't say that I agree, but I totally understand."

The two friends say their goodbyes to one another, agreeing to see each other again the next morning. Chris watched as Vicky went into her house. He was so full of love and admiration for her, only wishing he could tell her how he really felt, desperately wanting to reach out, hold her tight, and tenderly press his lips to hers.

When Vicky entered the quiet house, she saw her mother sitting in her favorite wingback chair, reading her Bible. After putting her books down, she hesitantly walked over to Monica, hugged and kissed her, and asked how her day was.

"Hey, Baby girl, my day was fine, but tell me, how was your day?" Monica responded, placing her Bible in her lap, excited to hear what her daughter had to say. Her mood was always lifted when Vicky was around.

Vicky looked down at her shoes, feeling nervous about bringing up the topic of going to college. Still, she knows she can't keep it to herself. "Well, Mom... it was really good. I met with Mrs. Carter, my school counselor, today, and she told me that because of my 3.9 GPA and my art skills, I qualify for a scholarship."

"Vicky, that's wonderful!" her mother exclaimed. Despite the unreliable support from Andre over the years, she still wanted the best possible outcome for her daughter. "I just got off the phone with Mrs. Carter, and she told me you're not sure about what you want to do," she said, concern crossing her face.

Vicky was surprised that Mrs. Carter had already called about the scholarship. Thinking back on her conversation with Chris, she was relieved that she had decided to have this conversation with her mom.

"We had a long talk," Monica continued. "She had nothing but good things to say about you. So, why don't you tell me why you don't feel ready to go to college?"

"Mom, I've decided that I am going to college; I'm just going to work for a couple of years so that I can save some money and help you out along the way."

Monica's emotions were no longer concealed as tears

rolled down her face. Her daughter found a new way every day to make her proud. "Do you know how much I love you?" she asked. "Baby, you don't have to worry about me; I'm going to be just fine. But you're practically grown now, so I'm going to let you make your own decisions. Now, if that is what you want to do, that's fine with me. I only hope that you don't wait too long before going to college."

Pleased that her mother was letting her take on the responsibilities as an adult, Vicky gave her the biggest hug ever. "Thank you, Momma. I love you!"

"I love you too, baby. I love you too!"

CHAPTER **SIX**

Vicky's graduation day was one of Monica's happiest memories. Sitting in the crowd alongside her closest friends, she cried with joy, brimming with pride at her baby's accomplishments. The students received their diplomas one by one, walking across the stage, smiling and waving at loved ones in the crowd. Once they had all crossed, they came together and tossed their hats into the air to celebrate what they had achieved.

Two years have passed since the day of graduation, and Vicky found herself working a monotonous job at Starbucks. She is now twenty years old and still lives at home with her mother. Each day for her is a dull routine: taking orders, making coffee, taking money, and giving change before going home and doing it all again the next day.

Standing around 5' 10" inches tall with perfectly toned legs that look amazing in heels, Vicky is beautiful. Her skin is radiant and the color of soft caramel; her hair is brown with streaks of natural highlights. As she looked up to take an order from the next customer, her eyes met those of a man who appeared to be in his mid-twenties. He was smiling at her with a double row of straight white teeth, and she thought it to be one of the nicest smiles she had ever seen.

"Hello, Vicky... can I have a cafe grande mocha latte, please?" he asked.

As he told her what he would like, she realized she couldn't stop smiling. "Sure, right away," she replied. Then, realizing that he had called her by her name, she paused and asked, "Have we met before? How did you know my name?"

He winked at her and said, "Well... your name is pinned on your chest, and I must say, you wear it well."

Vicky felt herself blushing but tried to remain confident. "Are you flirting with me?"

"No, I just have good taste in my coffee and my women," he responded plainly.

"Real funny. Well, it isn't fair that you know my name, and I don't know yours," Vicky replied, trying to play him at his own flirtatious game.

"Oh, I'm sorry… my name is Jarred."

Now shaking with nervous energy, Vicky served Jarred

his order and managed to spill coffee all over the countertop as she handed him the cup.

"Excuse me. I don't usually do that!" If she thought she was blushing before, she could really feel her cheeks and neck grow warmer now.

"It's okay. You can make it up to me," Jarred said quickly.

"Over dinner, right?"

"How did you guess?" Jarred replied. "Seriously though, can I call you later?"

Vicky felt slightly disappointed as she explained that she lived with her mother and wasn't used to having men calling her. She wasn't sure that her mother would understand such a situation. So, expecting Jarred to give up as soon as he realized he couldn't take things any further, Vicky got quiet. But instead, he handed her his card with his number on it.

"Whenever you want to spill something on me, give me a call, okay?" he said slyly.

Vicky can't help but smile. "Okay, I'll think about it."

Later that night, Vicky returned home following her shift and spent the evening with Monica as she normally did. As they sat in the living room talking, she shared about the guy she had met at work that day and that he asked her for her phone number.

Monica took a moment to respond. "Oh really.... Hmm,

I'm sure he's not the first man that has ever asked you for your number. So tell me, what was he like? Was he tall, dark, and handsome?"

Slightly surprised by her mother's curiosity, Vicky decided to be honest in her answer. "Yes, he actually was very attractive, quite charming, and there was something about him that was almost mesmerizing."

This brought on a response that more closely resembled the one Vicky had expected of her mother. "Lord, help this child. It sounds as though you've been approached by one of them talking salesmen. That's the kind of man that just wants to have sex with you, and then what? Gone in sixty seconds! Baby, you be careful. You didn't give that man your number, did you?"

Vicky found her mom's statement quite humorous, and she chuckled to herself. However, she couldn't believe that her mom was talking this way.

"No, I didn't give him my number..."

"Well, good... You never know these days. Little boys want to be playas just like their daddies."

"Anyway, I took his number instead."

"Well, you are a grown woman now, and I really can't tell you who you can or cannot see. And don't you be bringing home nobody's Mac Daddy or Baby Mama Drama! I'm going to tell you like my momma told me, 'Dating men is a lot like a game of checkers. You make one wrong move and you might get dumped.'"

"Moooooooom!" Vicky said, rolling her eyes.

"Just promise you'll be careful!"

Vicky obliged, and with that, her mother took her leave to get ready for bed. They said their goodnights, and Monica headed for the stairs. Once she was alone, Vicky took another look at the card given to her by Jarred and began to wonder if this guy would be worth the trouble. Then, tucking the card back into her pocket, she went upstairs to her room.

All night long, Vicky lay in bed tossing and turning with her phone in her hand, wanting to call Jarred but unable to dial all seven numbers before immediately hanging up. Finally, she fell into a fitful sleep that carried her through until the morning.

Three days later, Vicky was at work again, making the same coffees for the same sea of commuters and stay-at-home moms as she always did. When the morning rush was finally over, and she had a second to catch her breath, the bell on the door rang, notifying her that a customer had just walked in.

Busy cleaning up the workstation before the next rush of people, Vicky didn't lift her head to look at the customer. It was for this reason that she didn't realize that it was Jarred until she heard, "One cafe grande mocha latte, please..." in that voice that had been playing in her head for the past few days. She looked up to find Jarred ordering from her colleague at the register; he spotted her in seconds. "Oh... hi, Vicky," he said with that *incredible* smile.

Like the last time, Vicky couldn't help but smile back as he spoke to her. "Hi, Jarred. How've you been?" She said in the most casual tone of voice that she could manage.

"I'm fine, thanks for asking. How are you?"

"Pretty good. Just staying busy."

"Too busy to call?"

Vicky gave a small laugh at how forthright Jarred was — it was refreshing to be around someone who said what they were thinking. "No, I've been meaning to give you a call. I just keep getting side-tracked."

The conversation moves more quickly from this point, almost to the stage where Vicky can no longer keep up with it.

"Okay, are you busy tonight?" Jarred fired back.

"No, I'm not busy tonight."

"Good, I'll pick you up at, let's say... 8:00?"

"Wait, hold up. I- , I-, um, uh…"

Jarred is undeterred by Vicky's hesitation. "Would 7:00 be a better time?"

Vicky took a second to pause before replying, then said, "First of all, I need to know something."

"Okay, sure. What is it?"

"You need to let me know, and you have to answer honestly."

"Okay, of course…"

Vicky sighed before deciding to get it all out once and for all. "Are you a player or some kind of a pimp?"

Jarred smiled, then started to laugh. He couldn't

believe his ears. He continued laughing while Vicky stood there awkwardly, awaiting his answer. Finally composing himself, Jarred said, "No, come on now. No, I am not a Pimp."

"How 'bout a Player, are you a Playa'?" Vicky fired back at him; she was the one in control of the conversation now.

"No, I am not, nor have I ever wanted to be a Pimp or a Playa."

Vicky accepted this answer from him and gave him her address — letting him know not to be there any later than 8:05. He agreed and countered that he would be there no later than 7:50, which made Vicky laugh. She likes his sense of humor.

"Okay, cool... see you later. Don't work too hard," Jarred said with a wink, grabbing his coffee and heading for the door. But not before he brushed his shoulders off and pimped out of the coffee shop in jest.

CHAPTER **SEVEN**

True to his word, it was exactly ten minutes shy of 8:00 when Jarred rang the doorbell that night. He rang twice, prompting Vicky to jump up from where she was sitting. She was feeling a combination of nerves and excitement for what the evening had in store, but at this precise moment, her priority was making it to the front door before her mother did. Opening the door, she was happy to see Jarred's handsome face on the other side.

"Hey Jarred, I see that you made it right on time. And I do mean *right* on time," Vicky said, looking at her watch to confirm the time.

"Well, I only ran through every light and stop sign in the neighborhood just to get here on time," Jarred responded in his usual joking tone.

"That was very careless of you... my mom would like to meet you all in one piece."

"Okay, sure. I would love to meet her as well!"

Vicky was now smiling with puppy dog eyes and escorted Jarred into the living room, offering him a seat as she began to call for her mother to come downstairs and meet someone.

At the sound of her daughter shouting for her, Monica was startled, prompting her to run out of the kitchen with a knife in her hand, thinking there might be some sort of trouble. "Vicky, what's wrong, baby? Why are you yelling... is everything okay?"

Surprised to see her mother coming out of the kitchen, Vicky momentarily hesitated before replying. "Oh, Mom! I'm sorry... I thought you were upstairs. I was only trying to get you to come down and meet Jarred."

It took Vicky a second to notice the butcher's knife in her mother's hand. She grinned and then jokingly asked, "Mom, what are you doing with that knife?"

"Well, all I heard was yelling. I didn't know what was going on out here. I can't take no chances and let anything happen to my baby," Monica replied, lowering the knife to her side.

"Mom, this is Jarred — the guy I was telling you about the other day."

"Oh, I'm sorry! Forgive my manners. It's nice to meet you, Jarred."

"It's a pleasure to meet you as well, Ma'am," Jarred replied. Unphased by all the commotion he had just witnessed, he remained his charming and calm self.

Monica sat down in the living room so that she could better interrogate Jarred and smiled as she took a seat in her favorite Lazy-Boy chair. Vicky could tell that the questioning was about to begin; she knew her mother would take no prisoners.

"So, Jarred... if you don't mind, why don't you tell me a little something about yourself, like who's your parents, are you married, any baby mama drama, do you got a job, a dog, a cat, and last but not least, are you a pimp?"

Jarred smiled, which Vicky took as a positive sign — he didn't appear to be deterred by any of this. He simply responded to everything that her mother asked. "Well, my parents are Wilma and Charlie Parker. No, I'm not married, no dogs, no cats... three different baby mamas, though." He paused before breaking into a smile. "Gotcha, I'm just kidding.... and no, Ma'am, I ain't no pimp. Why does everybody keep asking me that?" He said, laughing.

Monica smiled at him, but she wasn't done just yet. "Well, good. I just need to let you know one thing... if you ever hurt my baby, boy, I'll cut you!" she stated, waving the knife in her hand. "I will gut you like a fish, and I will castra-"

"Mooooooom!" Vicky interrupted, embarrassed at the turn this conversation had taken.

"I'm just kidding, but I ain't playing...." Monica says in a warning voice, continuing to point the knife toward Jarred, simultaneously making a joke and letting him know she is deadly serious.

"No, Ma'am, you don't have to worry about me... I would never do anything to hurt your daughter. Absolutely nothing."

Monica raised one eyebrow. "And I have your word on that?"

"Yes, Ma'am, Jarred replied confidently.

"Okay, Mom... Jarred and I are going to go out for a little bit," Vicky interjected, trying her best to put an end to Monica's questioning.

Monica missed the cue that her daughter was trying so desperately to communicate. "Oh, well... okay... where you two off to? Are you taking my baby to a nice restaurant? What's the number to where you're going? Let me see your driver's license… do you have a 401k?"

"Mother!" exclaimed Vicky, exasperated that her mother was unrelenting — not letting them leave nor leaving the poor man alone.

Jarred remained undisturbed by the interrogation. "With your permission, Ma'am, I would like to take Vicky to dinner and maybe a movie." He didn't indulge her other questions but managed to say just the right thing to appease her.

Monica sighed and leaned back in her chair; she had finally heard enough from this man to trust him, although not entirely, to take her daughter out on a first date. "Just as long as you have her home within a reasonable time and you two don't get into any trouble, then yes, you have my permission."

Vicky, now excited and entirely relieved that her mother had given her permission to go out with Jarred and impressed that Jarred could keep his cool throughout her questioning, hugged and kissed her mother.

During the brief embrace, Monica took the opportunity to whisper in her daughter's ear. "He's cute, but you watch him closely and be careful."

Vicky knew that everything her mother did for her, frustrating though it might be, came from a place of love and protection. However, she wasn't willing to give her a chance to go any further in this particular moment, so rather than responding, she broke off the hug and gave a cheery, "Bye, Mom!" And with that, Vicky and Jarred can finally leave the house together. Vicky let out a sigh of relief and followed him to his car.

Once they had parked outside the restaurant, Jarred got out of the car first and walked around to open Vicky's door for her. She's impressed; he has acted nothing but gentlemanly since leaving her mother's house. As she stepped out of the vehicle, she realized they were outside a fancy French restaurant she had passed by but had never been in. She didn't express it, but she had to admit to herself that she was impressed by his venue choice.

Holding the door open for her, Jarred allowed her to step inside before him, and immediately, the two of them were surrounded by candlelight and a cozy red interior. As Vicky looked around in admiration, the hostess approached them within a matter of seconds, two elegant menus in hand and ready to seat them at their table. Jarred and Vicky followed closely behind her.

Arriving at their intimate table for two, Jarred pulled out the chair for Vicky to sit down on as she continued to look around, thinking how nice this restaurant was. She's never been anywhere like this to eat before, and, if she was being entirely honest with herself, she was a little nervous and starting to feel a little underdressed in this very classy establishment.

Once they were both seated, the hostess handed them their menus and asked them in French whether there was anything she could get for them. Jarred instantly responded. “Pouvez-vous nous apporter la carte des vins, s'il vous plaît?”

In utter amazement that Jarred appeared to speak fluent French, yet not knowing what the hostess had asked or his reply, Vicky smiled and turned to Jarred. "Wow, I'm impressed! So, tell me what she said to you, and what did you say to her?"

"Oh, she simply asked if we will be making love under the stars tonight-"

Vicky choked on her water as she was taking a sip, looking at Jarred in disbelief while also letting out a slightly embarrassed laugh. She could feel herself starting to blush.

"No, seriously, she asked if we wanted anything else, and I asked if she could bring us their finest wine list."

Still in a state of disbelief at the interaction that she had just witnessed, Vicky worked to keep her cool while asking Jarred more about this. Okay, I never would have guessed that you spoke another language. Are there any other languages that you speak?

"Well, I also speak a little Japanese, Swahili, and Spanish, and I am slowly learning Chinese."

"That's impressive! Where did you learn to speak more than one language? Was one of your parents French or something?"

Jarred smiled at her, happy to continue the conversation effortlessly and pleased that she was taking so much of an interest in him. "No, I was a business major at Stanford, and my counselor insisted that I learned more than one language, so it is now my goal to learn at least five languages."

"Well, okay... you go, boy!" Vicky exclaimed.

This makes Jarred laugh — he is enamored by her candid nature. "Well, thank you, I will take that as a compliment," he said, explaining that after attending Stanford, he landed a prestigious job at a large financial firm in Tennessee. He was young, ambitious, and financially stable. Well on his way to fulfilling his five-year plan that he carefully mapped out.

Vicky picked up the menu and, upon seeing that it was written in French, closed it and laid it back down on the table. She knew there was really no point in trying to decipher anything on it since she couldn't read a word of French. Jarred offered to translate the menu for her.

"No, that's okay. Why don't you just go ahead and order for me."

"Are you sure?"

"Yes, I trust you… I'm not going to learn French in an hour, but I'll trust that you will teach me a little later," Vicky said, slightly flirtatious.

The waiter came over to the table a few minutes later, introduced himself as Pier, and asked them, thankfully in English this time, if they were ready to order. Jarred confirmed that they were and proceeded to continue the conversation in French, telling Pier both of their names before stating what they would like to eat.

Before Pier left the table, Jarred directed a question to Vicky. "Oh, I am so sorry, Vicky. I have just ordered you a Filet Mignon. You do eat beef, right?"

Vicky smiled at his thoughtfulness. "Yes, that will be fine. Just make sure it's cooked well done."

"But of course," he replied before returning to his conversation with Pier providing Pier with Vicky's final instructions and then telling him that this would be all for now.

"Ah yes, monsieur... as you have requested. I shall have our finest chef prepare the two of you the most delectable meal ever," Pier replied, stomping his foot once, clapping his hands twice, kissing his fingertips, and throwing his hand in the air before gracefully walking away.

As Pier departed, the hostess returned with the wine list, handing it to Jarred, who took a cursory look and handed it back, saying, "Bring me your finest bottle of red wine, please. Spare no expense... I only want the sweetest and the best wine in your cellars." Only, to Vicky's utter delight, he said it entirely in French.

CHAPTER **EIGHT**

Vicky remained impressed with the efforts that Jarred was making and was dying to get to know more about him. "So, Jarred... you mentioned that you went to Stanford. How was it?"

Jarred was happy to continue engaging in the easy conversation he found himself in with Vicky. "It was great... it was a lot of hard work, but I met a lot of great friends and learned a lot. Thanks to my years at Stanford, I've been able to excel in my business career at my current job. But please tell me, are you working your way through college right now, or have you already graduated?"

Vicky sighed before launching into the script that had become all too familiar to her. "Mmm... I'm' glad you asked. I'm working on it. As a matter of fact, I just enrolled at Tennessee State. I hear they have an excellent Africana Studies department. This way, I can kill two birds with one stone."

"Ah, TSU... great school... good choice. But what do you mean about two birds, one stone?"

"Well, my dad used to share some interesting ancestral knowledge with me, and I don't want to just throw away everything he taught me or my opportunity," Vicky replied, taking a sip from her water glass. "Not to mention, TSU is an HBCU, and I'm sure my dad will be proud of me. Also, I have a few scholarships to explore, and before they rescind the offer, I need to get the ball rolling. I only decided to put my plans on hold because my mom needed extra financial help."

Jarred pressed some more, fascinated by what Vicky planned to do with herself. "So, tell me, what will your major be?"

Vicky's face immediately lit up as she began to speak about her passion, and this did not go unnoticed by Jarred. "The love of my life is art. In my spare time, I love to draw and paint... there is so much comfort and relaxation in my work," she said excitedly.

Jarred smiled. Her enthusiasm was entirely contagious. "Wow, now that's impressive," he said before pausing for a minute as a thought crossed his mind. "Wait a minute, all of those beautiful paintings in your mother's house... did you paint those?"

Vicky nodded. "Yes, they're all my babies," she said proudly.

"Well, you definitely have a wonderful gift, and a talent such as yours should not be taken lightly. Make sure you pursue your career in art; it sounds like you're on the right track."

This made Vicky smile; it was nice to hear that someone else believed in her and her talents— even if it was someone she barely knew.

As Vicky and Jarred continued their conversation, the hostess brought them a bottle of wine and poured the first glass for them. Shortly afterward, their food arrived. When the waiter removed the tops from the dishes, steam instantly filled the air.

"Ah, exquisite, isn't it?" Pier said, glancing between the two of them.

Neither Vicky nor Jarred was sure whether Pier was speaking about the food or the two of them, yet both secretly hoped it was the latter.

Months passed between Vicky and Jarred with the same promise, hope, and ease they had shared that first evening. The weeks passed like a dream, and the more that time went on, the more Vicky was absolutely convinced she was in love.

Sitting in Vicky's room together, laughing and talking as they always did and listening to music — they both loved Stevie Wonder's song "I Wish" — Vicky got a kick out of joking that Jarred's hair was probably nappy when the part came up about "looking back on when I was a little nappy headed boy." Jarred, amused by Vicky's words, would tickle her, and as the song followed with, "Then my only worry was for Christmas, what would be my toy?" Vicky would respond, "I ain't your toy!"

Monica, upon arriving home, knocked on the door and yelled, "Hey! Turn the music down!"

Vicky opened the door slowly, giggling and apologizing to her mother, but Monica was not amused. With an "I'm going to kill you" gaze, she looked Vicky right in the eyes and said, "Look, what have I told you about playing music so loud in my house? Oh, and I know that ain't Jarred in there, is it? I thought I told you that man is up to no good." Monica was getting more and more irate by the second. "Lord, help this child."

Vicky felt exasperated by how her mother was reacting. She couldn't understand why Monica couldn't just be happy for her. "Look, Mom... I'm not a little girl anymore. You need to put more trust in me."

Monica replied with the same thing she always did when she and Vicky had this conversation. "The only person I trust is the Lord."

Vicky knew that she should stop talking, apologize to her mother, and put the conversation to bed, but it all came tumbling out of her mouth before she could do anything to stop it. "Mom, you are always talking about the Lord. Sometimes I wonder if you are just praying to keep men away. Ever since Dad left you, you have been-"

Vicky wasn't given a chance to finish what she was going to say before Monica shouted, "How dare you!" and felt the intense sting of an unexpected slap across her face.

"You watch your tone with me, young lady," Monica said, angry and showing no sign of regret for what she had done. She then turned away from Vicky and walked down the stairs.

Vicky was suspended in a state of total shock and disbelief at the horrible fight that had just happened between her and her mother. She couldn't understand why she had never been able to mention her father leaving and why they could never speak about it together or why it led to this kind of argument when she tried to. Having said that, she and Monica had never fought like this before... this was new for her.

In her state of anger, frustration, and hurt, Vicky contemplated leaving the only security blanket she had ever known — home with her mother.

Returning to her room, she began to cry on Jarred's shoulder.

"Is everything okay? What was all that about?" he asked.

Vicky tried to dry her tears as she collected her thoughts and attempted to summarize all of the complicated feelings she had toward her mother. "All I ever wanted was for my mother to be happy. I stayed out of school to help her, and she still doesn't understand me." This was the best she could do while all the emotions were still so raw. How could her mother treat her this way? After everything she was trying to do for her.

Jarred hugged Vicky tightly and tried his best to comfort her; he wanted to say whatever it took to make things better for Vicky. "Look, if you want to, you can always stay at my place."

Despite the voice in her head telling her that it was too soon or that she should stick around to try and sort things out with her mother, Vicky took Jarred up on the offer and began packing a few things. As she made her way through the house, she saw her mother in the kitchen, cutting onions and crying. Immediately feeling terrible at the sight of her mother in pain, Vicky placed her overnight bag at the door and walked over to where Monica was standing.

"I'm sorry, Mom. I don't want things to be this way, but right now, I just need a little space. Jarred and I are in love, and I need to learn how to breathe on my own for a change."

"Don't you think you're moving too fast?" Monica sniffed, drying her tears.

"Fast or slow, Mom... I got to learn how to breathe for me."

At that moment, Monica and Vicky heard the horn of Jarred's car blowing; they simultaneously turned their heads toward the sound.

Vicky looked into her mother's tearful eyes and, in a soft, somber voice, whispered, "I love you, Mom."

Monica sighed slowly. "I love you, too," she said, pulling Vicky in for a tight hug. "Be careful, Baby. Be really careful."

Vicky hugged her mother back and kissed her on the cheek before turning towards the door to meet Jarred outside.

CHAPTER **NINE**

Over the next six months, Vicky stayed at Jarred's in order to try living away from her mother for the first time in her life. This evening had gone like most other nights since they had been living together. Vicky was sitting on the couch in the living room, waiting for Jarred to come home. She heard his car pull up out front and park, waited the typical three or four minutes, and then heard him stumble in the door — drunk and tiptoeing like a little kid. Vicky spoke loudly and clearly.

"Really? This is why you had me move out of my mom's house? So that you could ignore me? Baby, we gave it a try; but this isn't working for either one of us. For the past six months, you've been going out almost every night of the week."

Her voice was enough to startle Jarred in his drunken haze. "You're right," Jarred slurred back. "I made your mother a promise. I said I would never hurt you, and that's the least I will do... Vicky, I just want you to know that you didn't do anything wrong. Maybe I'm some of those things or all those things you said I was."

"I'll be out by the end of the week," Vicky replied in the same measured tone.

"No, baby, you don't have to go anywhere. I have another place on the other side of town. You can stay here as long as you like; just make sure you pay the mortgage."

"I figured that. You could have told me, Jarred. I'm a big girl, you know... I can handle it. Now, there's the couch, and I expect you will be gone in the morning." She knew that being firm about this matter was the only way to go about it. She didn't have the time or the energy to bring her emotions into this.

Jarred sighed, looking slightly defeated. "Well Damn.... Okay, baby. I hear ya." Early the following morning, Jarred cleared out most of his personal belongings, leaving Vicky alone.

Vicky didn't call her father often; when she did, Andre would always detect that something wasn't going as planned. Still, she decided it was time to call him.

"Hello, Dad."

"Are you okay?" Andre replied.

"Yes, I just needed to hear your voice."

Deep down, Andre knew Vicky was responding to her living arrangements based on his past discrepancies, so he didn't want to criticize her unjustly, but he did not hold back by letting her know that living with a guy at her young age was not a great idea.

One of Andre's favorite songs was "God Bless the Child" by Stevie Wonder. The song resonated in his heart and exemplified hope for his one and only daughter, even if she considered herself grown. He reminded her that God gave her a gift, and if she didn't use it correctly, she would lose it indirectly.

Not liking the way the conversation was going, Vicky interrupted him. "Dad, please... not now." She told her father that she would talk with him later and abruptly hung up the phone.

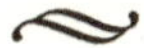

Vicky pulled up beside her mother's house and parked her car. Before unbuckling her seatbelt, she sat for a second and sighed; she couldn't quite believe this was happening. Bracing herself for the interaction, Vicky got out of the car and approached the front door. She used the key around her neck to go inside and look for her mother.

Walking into the living room of her former home, Vicky saw Monica kneeling and realized that her mom was praying. She backed up slowly towards the front door, opened it, and slammed it harder to let her mom know she had come to visit. The sound was enough to bring Monica out of her prayer.

"Vicky, is that you, baby?"

"Yes, Mom. How are you?"

Monica paused for a second, sighed, and then responded, "Baby, I'm fine; just batting with the Lord. Just battling with the Lord."

Vicky hesitated and then said what she had come to say. "Mom, you were right; it's been rough out there-"

Monica looked at her daughter with sympathy and concern — and a hint of *I told you so.* "Just remember what I had to go through."

Vicky knew this part had been inevitable, but she needed her mother right now, and nothing was going to change that. "I know, Mother… I know… I just wanted to stop by and visit. What's for dinner?"

"Dinner? I have a date! Just kidding. It's Wednesday night, so you know I've got bible study; I have a date with God. But I can whip up something for us right quick. A little baked hen, pinto beans, macaroni and cheese, sweet potatoes, collard greens, and little girrrl… you know I'm known for my award-winning hot-water cornbread."

They both laughed at Monica's joke as they walked into the kitchen, settling for leftover meatloaf from the night before.

That night Vicky was feeling restless and deep in her thoughts. She couldn't sleep, so she decided to do what she often did at times like these, driving through the streets at night to try to clear her head. There was something so peaceful about the world when it was dark out with no one around. Plus, she had a lot to think about.

Vicky was in deep thought as she drove. Reliving the feeling of separation that had previously happened to her own mother during her divorce from her father, Vicky submitted herself to re-establishing the one thing that allowed her to express her innermost being — Art. Remaining in the apartment and maintaining her job at Starbucks would finally enable her to pursue her dreams. Her situation might not be perfect, but she knew in her heart that she was on the road to where she needed to be.

Vicky was on her way home but wasn't ready to face the empty apartment. Instead, she decided to take the scenic route to have some more time in this strange, nocturnal limbo that she treasured so much as a reprieve from her life.

While driving, she became aware of the faint sound of music coming from somewhere up ahead. Intrigued, she rolled the window down fully to discover that it was coming from inside a brownstone brick building. Pulling up, she saw that it was a jazz club called "Jazzy Blues" that she had heard of before, located in the historical part of town. *What the heck!* she thought to herself as she got out of the car to go inside.

Vicky entered the club and immediately liked what she heard; the music was lively but soothing at the same time, and the people inside the club were simply enjoying what the musicians had to offer. More importantly, Vicky's heart did not waver as she pulled her large sketch pad from her bag and began doing what she loved more than anything in the world. Before long, she had captured on paper the very essence of the musicians' movements, spirit, and eloquence.

Vicky didn't even notice until she was nearly done that a crowd had gathered around her, watching her sketch the band in awe and whispering to one another how impressive they found her. Looking at the group of people around her, Vicky noticed a man who didn't break his stare for even a second. In a mesmerized state, he seemed like he could not have stopped even if he wanted to. But finally, he walked over and introduced himself.

"Hello," he said in a deep voice.

"Hi," Vicky responded.

"Can I help you with anything?"

"You can help me find the owner of this club," Vicky answered, wanting to speak to whoever owned this wonderful establishment.

The man's voice, even smoother than before, replied, "As a matter of fact, he sent me over here to talk to you; he wanted to know what you were drawing and why you had the crowd so aroused?"

"Oh, I was just sketching for my next painting. So, you know the owner?"

The man smiled but did not show any teeth. "Quite well, actually. Would you like to meet him?"

"Very much so."

"Why don't you follow me..." he said, walking Vicky toward the corner of the bar and leading her into a beautifully decorated office. "He will be right in to speak with you."

Vicky walked through the door and sat down. Once inside, the man immediately left. Vicky looked around and saw the lavish office was filled with well-known autographed pictures of world-renowned contemporary jazz and blues musicians. It was impressive; whoever the owner was had obviously been in the industry for a while and had met everyone there was to know in jazz.

The man returned to the office with a couple of drinks and sat in the plush chair in front of Vicky. He was short in stature and appeared to be in his early forties. Although he had a dark chocolate complexion with a clean, shaved head, his voice carried with strong conviction. His build was muscular; it appeared he worked out often. Although quite helpful, there was something peculiar about his crooked smile.

Vicky was growing frustrated at this interaction. She didn't want to be left in an office, and she didn't want to sit here and have drinks with a perfect stranger. "Look, Mister. I appreciate the drink, but I really would like to talk to the owner."

The man held his hands up in surrender, amused at her small outburst. "Hold on... You're looking at him. Please, call me Terrell."

Vicky was embarrassed at having harassed this man when he was the one she was looking for, after all. "You're good," she said, laughing and trying to make light of the situation. "I'll admit it; you got me… I'm sorry, I don't think I properly introduced myself. My name is Vicky Alexander. Am I in trouble or something? I mean, is there a fee to sketch or paint here?"

"No, not for you," Terrell replied. "You should never be paying; you're really good, and people should be paying you. Actually, I have some ideas and think you might be a good fit for the club. Wait… you are old enough to drink, right?"

"It didn't stop you from asking me before," Vicky answered. She then quickly thought *maybe this guy wasn't so bad after all.*

The same voice that sounded deeper than the ocean was now making waves. "So, can I call you to discuss this business proposition over dinner?" Terrell looked serious; he really meant what he was saying.

Vicky knew enough by this point to be slightly wary of propositions like this, but she wasn't about to turn down an opportunity to be paid for her art, so she said, "Okay, I guess that will be okay. Do you have something that I can write my number down on?"

"Do you have a business card?"

"No, I'm just getting started."

"I tell you what... I can help you with all that. By the way, how much would you like to sell that sketch for?"

Vicky gave Terrell a mischievous smile, "I don't think you can afford it…"

They were still laughing at the encounter as they stood up from their chairs and began to leave. No sooner had they left the office than one of the band members approached them. Vicky expected that the band member would have a question for Terrell. To her surprise, he immediately directed his question at Vicky, "Hey, how much would you be willing to sell the sketch for?"

Vicky hesitated for a moment, then she started to speak, with no real idea what she would reply regarding the price of her sketch. "Well, drawing and sketching is my passion-"

Terrell, on the other hand, who was much older and experienced than she was, with a dog-eat-dog world attitude from time spent in the industry, stepped right in and interrupted her,

"-Leon, If you want to see more of Vicky's work, you need to speak directly with me. Her prices start at $350 and up."

Vicky took notice of Terrell's demeanor, but she didn't say anything. Her key focus was the number that had just come out of Terrell's mouth; it was big... one that she could use in her bank account right now.

She tried to adopt the same hardness she had just witnessed, "Well, you heard the man."

"Uh, I'll get at you later after a couple more paychecks," replied the band member before he turned and walked away.

By now, both Vicky and Terrell's wheels were turning; they both just realized that there might be a market for her work. Terrell did not waste a second beating around the bush,

"Young lady, seriously… How would you like to set up here weekly? We can do a 60/40 split."

"Who gets the sixty, and who gets the forty?" Vicky replied.

"Let me think about it," Terrell said with a silly smirk. "Just kidding. You'll get to keep sixty. I will call you tomorrow."

Vicky realized she could finally make up for the lost rent from Jarred with the kind of money that she would be able to make here. She decided right then to seal the deal with a handshake.

CHAPTER **TEN**

Everything in Vicky's life had been utterly turned around in the following months. She had gone from mourning her breakup with Jarred while struggling to make ends meet by working at Starbucks to dating Terrell and becoming one of the main attractions in the city. People went mad for her sexy eyes, and they loved how her hair always seemed to sway to the music as she danced along with the rhythm of the beat.

Vicky had become quite the hot commodity a man loved to keep around, and she had brought countless people to the club to watch her paint. Similar to a baton twirler, she had learned to twirl the brushes — a skill she had taught herself but had mastered to a tee. But at this moment, Vicky was sitting on the couch, painting her toenails.

The phone started to ring, and she maneuvered herself to answer it. "Hello?"

It was Terrell on the other end. "Hello, boo."

"Hello," Vicky repeated.

"Hey, babe. Where are you? I think you might wanna come in today."

"What's up? I thought I would take today off. I've been working non-stop for months now. I'm not feeling that well." It was true; Vicky had rarely had a night off since she started working at the Jazz club. She needed at least one night to recharge and feel less burned out.

Terrell responded almost as if he didn't hear her at all. "A new band is coming in, and they are good. I think you will be able to vibe with them. Try to get here before 7:00."

Vicky sighed, she had never been good at saying no to people, and to make matters worse, Terrell was not someone who was easy to say no to. He was persuasive and used to getting exactly what he wanted, which meant that Vicky had gotten used to giving him just that — a fact both her parents despised. After all, Vicky was a free spirit. She had trouble listening to anything that didn't make sense outside the stroke of the brush. She loved art and would do almost anything to keep her creative flow from being jeopardized, even if it meant pretending with Terrell.

"Okay, I guess I can make it down there before the show starts," Vicky conceded, hanging up the phone and getting herself ready.

But, once she got outside to her car, she realized that she had a flat tire. Knowing this would cause a delay, and that Terrell would be furious at her for being late, she decided to call a cab. Luckily, most of the paint supplies she needed were already at the club, so she only carried the good sable brushes with her, the kind that made the paint flow like water to a river.

Vicky arrived at the club and immediately noticed Terrell staring at her and tapping his watch as if to say, "you're late." She gave him an exasperated look as she desperately put her hands up. As she was setting up, she recognized one of the band members. Vicky couldn't believe that it was really him. "Oh, my Goodness! How are you doing?"

It was Chris, now in his early twenties and still quite handsome with a head full of thick bushy hair that appeared to fit a musician's persona. "Vicky! How are you, sweetheart? What are you doing here?" he said with a look of pure joy on his face.

"I'm painting here tonight. I'm an artist." It still felt surreal to her to say those words out loud. She could barely contain the smile on her face whenever she told someone. Saying it to Chris felt even better, knowing how much he had believed in her all those years ago.

Chris looked as impressed as she would have expected. "Oh, so you're the one I've been hearing so much about. Sorry, dear... I had no idea it was you. It's good to see that you are still pursuing your dreams. Hey, let's talk after the show."

Terrell was watching from a distance but read Chris's lips as “Sweetheart” came out with a grin from ear to ear showing nothing but clean white teeth. A possessive man who didn't like his women to have wandering eyes, when he caught Vicky staring and waving at someone in the band before she had properly greeted him, he instantly became upset. His dominating personality rising to the surface, he rushed over to interfere in their conversation.

"Is everything okay?"

"Chris is an old childhood friend," Vicky offered with a sparkle in her eyes. "We go way back!"

Terrell looked exasperated. "Okay… but isn't the show about to start? We have a full house, and I'm not paying the band to stand around and talk. Chris, you're on in five minutes... you too, Vicky. Shouldn't you be setting up your paintbrushes or something?"

Chris smiled and walked off. Vicky started to do the same, but Terrell grabbed her. "Hey, how far back do you and your childhood friend go?"

Vicky knew immediately where this was going. "Let's not do this right now. I'm getting ready to start painting, and you are messing with my flow."

Terrell walked away, angry and jealous. The band began to play, and the crowd got wound up with excitement. Vicky loved the vibe from the new band, and the sound was incredible. Chris played the saxophone as if he was catering a solo just for Vicky. She started to sway from side to side; her hands and hips were all in the moment as she painted a masterpiece during the set. To her delight, Vicky had no problem selling the painting for $1,000 right after the show. Terrell took half of this, of course, as he was accustomed to doing — not exactly a 60/40 split they had agreed upon before.

After the set, while the band was packing up and getting ready to leave, Chris came over to talk to Vicky. "Are you dating that guy?" he asked.

"Something like that," Vicky replied awkwardly.

Chris's protective instincts over Vicky immediately kicked in. "Something like what? He's very controlling. No, I stand corrected; he's out of control — a control freak."

Vicky went with what she usually did when someone confronted her about Terrell's behavior... tried to laugh it off. "Shut up, silly. He'll be alright; nobody controls me-"

Chris realized he probably wouldn't get anywhere criticizing Vicky's boyfriend, so he took a different tact. "Hey, Vicky, you did an awesome job. You are as beautiful as I remember when we were friends back in the day. Do you think it will be okay If I call you sometime?"

Vicky is grateful to have a friend back in her life. Her life lately has been consumed by Terrell and this job; it's all she ever wanted, but it's nice to have someone who remembered her for who she was back then.

"I will call you," she countered, exchanging numbers with him.

"Please do... for anything," Chris replied, really meaning it. "Oh, Vicky... I knew it was something I meant to ask you. Do you know this guy named Jarred?" he asked before turning to leave.

Shocked to hear Jarred's name again after all this time, Vicky answered, "Yes… Do you know him?"

"We have a mutual acquaintance." Although men talk sh** all the time about former girlfriends, Chris now knew deep down that the rumors of how passionate a young artist named Vicky was had to be true. This only made him desire her more.

"Hmmm..." Vicky said, simply shrugging her shoulders. "Small world."

Terrell has now joined them again in their presence… He stood back but soon interjected himself into their conversation. "You can say that again. Everybody knows every damn body else in this town. You got about two minutes to wrap this thing up, and we're out of here," he said before walking away.

Both Vicky and Chris were amazed by his actions. However, Vicky was so used to this kind of unwarranted behavior that she could ignore the small comments from Terrell. As such, she returned to her conversation with Chris. "You mention that you know Jarred, and I know he's into finance, so what do you do other than play the sax?" asked Vicky.

Chris ignored the first part of her question but fired back with that cheeky smile Vicky remembered and recognized so well. "Let's see… I eat dinner and want you to join me sometime?"

This made Vicky giggle, and she tried to laugh off the unexpected, proposed dinner date, trying to change the subject a little while still keeping the conversation friendly. "You're sure you eating? You look a little thin to me," she teased.

"I've been a little stressed lately, but I'm coping. I also go to church almost every Wednesday night; you can join me for that too. Seriously, I study the Bible faithfully. I still see your mom at church, you know."

"Wait... What? And you never asked about me?" Vicky asked, pushing Chris's shoulder playfully.

"I was hoping our two worlds would somehow collide when the timing was right," Chris said, sounding wiser than Vicky remembered from their time being best friends in school.

"You mean like a divine intervention? To be honest, I never thought you would stick with church like that."

"So, you're not into the word?" Chris asked.

Vicky had to admit that she had not kept up with her faith as her mother and Chris had with theirs. "Well, my mom does try to encourage me every chance she gets. I do pick up my Bible every now and then when she isn't looking," she replied in a hesitant, slow voice.

From across the room, their conversation was interrupted again by Terrell snapping his fingers and hollering with a few choice cuss words in between.

"Hey, Vicky! Let's go..."

Vicky was at the end of her patience with Terrell at this point. First, he made her come to work on her night off, and then he wouldn't even let her catch up with her oldest friend. Forget it. Vicky meant what she had said to Chris earlier — no one controlled her or what she did but herself. As such, she continued to talk with Chris, which only provoked Terrell, who had come back over and grabbed her arm much more harshly than before.

"Hold up, man!" Chris shouted.

Vicky quickly motioned for Chris to stay back, yet she was outraged. "Hold on! I've asked you not to do that again."

"What have I told you about running your mouth, trying to make me look bad in front of other people?" Terrell was furious now. But once again, this was not uncommon in their relationship.

"You know what… I'm not feeling this. More importantly, I'm not feeling you," Vicky stated angrily. At times she wanted to believe that his bark was bigger than his bite; now she was convinced that Terrell had an inferiority complex about his height and felt the need to show off in front of men much taller than he was to prove a point. Tonight though, he was clearly acting like a bully.

Terrell raised his voice as if he were auditioning for a hollering contest. "I'm going to say this one more time! Get your sh** together... and let's go!"

"I'm not going anywhere with you acting like this," Vicky shouted back. "But I am leaving... just not with you."

CHAPTER **ELEVEN**

Terrell laughed in Vicky's face, "So what you wanna do? You want to leave me now? After everything I've done for you. You go when I tell you to go!" His face was contorted into a thunderous fury now. Terrell wasn't used to not getting what he wanted when he wanted it, especially when speaking to a woman.

Chris started to step in and come to Vicky's defense, but Vicky was dead set on handling this her way as she again motioned for Chris to stay back.

"I got this," she said to Chris without taking her eyes off Terrell. "You know what, Terrell? You might own this club, but guess what? You don't own me!" Vicky said forcefully. She had finally come to the end of her tether. "I may have been your prize, Terrell, but I'm not your possession. Better yet, keep the money," she said, throwing what she had made for the night back in his face. "It looks like after I'm gone, you just might need it!"

Terrell wasn't ready to take no for an answer. "I told you that you were filling up some big girl's shoes, but the truth of the matter is you're not woman enough to handle a man like me. The clock just struck twelve, Miss Cinderella. You missed out on this prince. Now get your stuff... your orange pumpkin is waiting outside! And don't come back in here; you're done, finished... you're through! Artists like you come a dime a dozen."

This time, Chris stepped in, not caring if he would get kicked out or rolled out in a body bag. He didn't care who this guy was. He wasn't putting up with anyone speaking to Vicky that way. "Hey, man! You really need to chill."

Terrell turned his anger onto Chris. "Little Boy Blue, you came to blow your horn? You were paid; now, you're done... both of you need to leave my club!"

"You no good scum of the earth!" Chris replied, and then, out of nowhere, Chris' fist landed a left hook to Terrell's mouth, knocking an already crooked tooth right out.

"You messed up now, young blood!" Terrell shouted, lunging into Chris with the weight of five punches. "You have no idea who you're dealing with!"

The two men continued to scuffle while Vicky repeatedly screamed, "Stop it! Stop it, please!" However, neither one listened or cared enough about her squeals as they violently punched and pounded on one another. Soon, Terrell's energy was exhausted, and he was suddenly knocked upside the head with a chair. He stumbled as he went down yet somehow managed to clip Chris' legs right from under him, and he too fell hard on the decorative concrete floor now spattered with both their blood.

As they swapped punches, it seemed they were playing tug-of-war as they pushed and pulled each other from one side of the club to the next. Terrell appeared to be losing the battle and kept talking trash even as Chris landed a solid punch to his nose. "Damn, dude! You broke my nose! No, you didn't... you wanna be John Coltrane, you and that fake Mona Lisa can get to steppin!"

This tirade only made Chris even angrier, and he slung Terrell clear over the bar — you could now hear the sound of glass breaking mixed in with Vicky's screams for them to stop. "C'mon, Chris! Let's just go!" she hollered. "He's not worth it!"

As Terrell fell behind the bar, he tried thinking his way out of this losing bout. That's when he saw the 9mm tucked away on a low shelf. Grabbing it, Terrell stood on the broken glass, looked directly at Chris, and pulled the trigger. However, the Glock jammed.

Adrenaline pumping, Chris lunged, dislocating Terrell's shoulder and causing the gun to fall loose from his grasp.

Just then, one of the bartenders attempted to call the police. But Terrell motioned for her to put the phone down as a muscular security member finally came through the front door. Terrell wasn't even sure why he had security. They constantly flirted with the guests and pretended to clear the parking lot outside after each show. Security had missed the altercation but was ready to escort Terrell's unwanted guests out of the club. But Chris did not back down.

"Hey, man," he said. "Don't start none... won't be none!"

Although he would do anything to defend Vicky at this point, Chris was no match for a fresh bout with someone who appeared to resemble Brutus from Popeye. So, Chris started to help Vicky pack up a few of her belongings, and the pair quietly exited the jazz club, leaving many of her things behind. What they couldn't grab fast enough, Terrell had security throw out onto the parking lot grounds.

Still trying to come to terms with what had just happened, Vicky felt a strange mixture of despair and relief. She didn't know what this would mean for her and her career, but she found comfort in the fact that Terrell wouldn't be in her future. Then, when it dawned on her that she hadn't driven due to her flat tire, she felt further relief upon seeing that Chris had an SUV, which had more than enough room to get mostly everything —damaged or not — packed into his vehicle.

Havoc had embarked on the night, and Chris offered to take her home so they could carefully sort through it. Despite everything that had gone down, Vicky was relieved knowing she had found her best friend again.

The pair sat in complete silence on the drive home. Chris instinctively knew that Vicky needed a bit of time to work through what had just happened; This would be a big change for her to come to terms with. They both appeared to be in some form of shock. Chris pulled up to drop Vicky off and looked over at her sitting in the car's passenger seat. He expected her to say her goodbyes and for him to give her a hand with her things, then he would go home.

Instead, Vicky finally broke her silence, saying, "I really appreciate you helping me. Would you like a drink?"

"No, ma'am! I don't drink."

Vicky laughed. "Lighten up... it's been a long night. How about a blunt? You know, a little reefer may relax both our minds."

"After all we been through tonight," Chris responded, "don't tempt me! But seriously, I'm good. And before you ask, It has nothing to do with my belief either; it messes with my throat. God gave me a gift, and I intend to use my talent of playing the sax for as long as He allows me to."

"Isn't it funny how life works," Vicky said. "All this time, I haven't even seen you around town, and in one brief moment, you're back in my life as if you were walking me home again."

"With just a little extra baggage this time," Chris teased.

"Ohhhh, you still have jokes, I see! Seriously though, where did you learn how to fight like that? Didn't you use to get beat up when we were kids?"

They both laughed…

"Awwwwh, you got jokes, too," Chris said, nursing his bruised knuckles before sharing how a former martial arts teacher known as Montu had educated him on African Spirituality. "I don't know why the ministers don't teach it in the West. It's all biblical, also historical. However, enough of that for now... maybe I can explain more later," he said, his voice taking on a serious tone. "In life, you should always try to defend yourself and what you believe in."

Which is? Vicky asked.

"You will come to know it," he said softly.

Vicky had no idea what Chris was referring to. She had previously assumed he had forgotten about all the moments they had spent together as they went in divergent ways.

Chris smiled and continued, "God always knows what's best."

"I believe He does."

"See, you do believe."

Vicky laughed. "You know what I mean! Hey, what's in the black case?" she asked, changing the subject.

"Something for the world to read. Let me share a Scripture with you, Vicky."

"Right Now?!" Vicky replied, laughing in disbelief.

Chris remained serious. "What better time than now? When you're going through something, if not you, then who... and if not now, then when?"

After Chris had shared the passage from the Bible with Vicky, she started to break down and cry. "That was so beautiful... thank you for everything. Thank you for just being you," she said through her tears.

"I know you probably don't believe it, but you're going to be alright," Chris replied, consoling her. "Let me rephrase that... one day, you're going to be great. Hey, I want to give you something. The next time you're down and out... I mean, when you're feeling really low, I want you to put this CD in and play number 7. It will make you feel like the world has been lifted off your shoulders."

"You know I'm not a religious fanatic," Vicky said, taking the CD.

Chris gave her a soft smile, "Shhhh... just listen."

"Okay, okay."

Chris helped Vicky gather her belongings, and as much as he did not want to leave, he broke up the evening by looking at his watch. "Well, I must run, dear. You know I'm here for you if you need me."

Vicky smiled, grateful to have had Chris during this difficult evening. She knew she would have felt very alone if he hadn't been there. "I know you are."

The two hugged for a long time before Vicky finally pulled away.

CHAPTER **TWELVE**

The next morning, Vicky was cleaning the apartment, trying her best to distract herself from the happenings of the previous evening. While dusting, she came across a picture of her mother and pulled it close to her heart — remembering all the times her mother prayed. Breaking down, she fell to her knees and began to cry.

Vicky looked at the CD player and pushed track #7 as Chris had previously instructed. She was astonished by how the song made her feel. Suddenly, she was moved to paint. As she did so, she felt some higher hold come over her, and soon, she was crying in the middle of her living room. "Chris was right! He was right!" she cried out, as if in a trance of some kind, unaware of anything other than how the music transcended through her painting and herself.

She began praising God for being there for her,

shouting, "Thank You, Lord. Thank you. Hallelujah, Hallelujah!"

Just then, the phone rang, and Vicky was brought out of her trance. Still crying from the experience she'd just had, she picked up the receiver — her voice slightly cracking as she said, "Hello?"

To her surprise, it was Chris' voice that she heard on the other end of the phone. "Hello, Vicky... are you okay?"

"I don't know. I need you to come over... like right now," she sniffed.

Chris was worried. "What's wrong?"

"That's just it; nothing is wrong. For once, I feel like everything is right. Chris, please hurry!"

He recognized that sound… Vicky sounded joyous now. It was the sweet sound of someone who had just had a major breakthrough.

As soon as Chris' feet hit the pavement in front of her home, Vicky swung the door open to greet him. After hugging for a moment, he noticed a painting behind her; it was of two black praying hands with a pyramid in the background. Spiritually moved by it, he walked past Vicky to examine it more closely.

"Where did this come from?"

"I took your advice, and I played track 7. Something phenomenal and wonderful began to evolve. I felt a spiritual presence upon me that I have never felt before...

and was guided by strokes far greater than my capabilities and praise beyond my own level of comprehension and expectation."

"WOW! This is so unique," Chris replied, continuing to stare at the painting. "What are you going to do with it?"

"I'm not sure, maybe frame it or... maybe give it to my mother."

With excitement in his voice, Chris blurted out, "Vicky, I know a couple of art dealers in town. Perhaps we can set up a show for you and auction it off."

Relieved in her new-found faith in God, Vicky agreed and allowed Chris to take the painting with him, trusting that he would be responsible with her visual testimony.

Once Chris had put the painting in the back of the SUV, he sat in the driver's seat, checking twice to make sure that Vicky wasn't looking out of the window or hadn't followed him downstairs before pulling a pipe out of the glove compartment and attempting to light up. He knew that Vicky wouldn't forgive him if she knew the disturbing and deceitful truth about him — that he had a crack problem and hid behind the Bible so that no one would ever find out about it. Despite his compassion for Vicky, Chris was a junky.

He began to pray to himself as he fumbled with his kit, "Lord, please forgive me. Awh, man, I'm out. What am I going to do?" He knew he needed a fix as soon as possible;

he couldn't live without it. But how was he going to afford more? Earnings from one show only went so far, and he'd blown it already.

In his mirror, he caught sight of Vicky's painting and turned around to look at it as a dreadful idea began to form. As an addict, he didn't have much control over thoughts like these; all he knew was that he needed a fix and that he needed it fast. So, Chris decided to drive to a gallery in a well-to-do district before he could reason or talk himself out of it. Before he knew it, he was in the gallery and approaching the counter with the painting of the praying hands with him.

Chris noticed that along with the gallery owner, a curator was also in the building. Standing at the desk, he could hear what they were saying to one another... at least until the owner spotted him.

"How may I help you?" asked the owner.

Chris staggered and stuttered, realizing at this point that he wasn't prepared for what he was going to say. "Yea, I- I- I would like to speak to someone about putting a piece of work on consignment."

"Let's see what you have here..."

"Well, it's an original work. It's acrylic and a 48x60."

"Oh my… It's spiritually captivating. So, you are Victoria?"

Chris was becoming frustrated since all he could think about was getting the money and getting that fix. "Do I look like Victoria? I'm representing her. We have been f- f-friends for years," he said, fidgeting. He couldn't seem to stand still. "Look, mister... I'm here representing- Can you help me out? I- I mean, do we have a deal or not? I know it's worth at least $1,000."

"Are you okay?" the gallery owner asked. "You seem a little hyper."

Chris could feel his patience wearing thin the longer he stood there. "You don't have to be concerned about whether or not I have ADD. I'm okay."

Now, the gallery owner was also getting frustrated and felt like Chris was wasting his time. "Look around; this is an upscale gallery... my family has owned this gallery for nearly half a century. If we let every Tom, Dick, and Harry in here off the street posing to be the artist or representative, we wouldn't be here very long!"

At this point, the curator now stepped in and joined their conversation. "Excuse me. Did you say this is a painting by Victoria Alexander?"

"Yeah, Yeah," Chris replied, clearing his throat and correcting himself. "I mean… yes, sir."

"I'm a long-time admirer of her work," the curator said, reaching out to shake Chris' hand. "Let me take a look at it. It definitely has a certain something about it that even I can't explain... I simply can't."

Together Chris and the gallery owner looked at each other and said simultaneously, "Spiritually Captivating."

"Why yes... very!" the curator exclaimed in agreement. "Not sure what your motive is, but how about I take this painting off your hands right now? Here is $700. Take it or leave it."

"C'mon man, it's an original!"

"And you're not Victoria... and you probably don't have a bill of sale or Letter of Authenticity either... do you?" the curator said, with a slight grin.

"Gentlemen, please!" the gallery owner interjected. "There will be no side bargaining in this gallery." Then, holding out his hand to Chris, he said, "My commission, please. We take 40% here."

Chris looked at him incredulously, "40%? You didn't even want to do the deal."

"I didn't. But all sales here on our premises are final; we take 40% of the sale, and you keep 60%."

Chris now had to give the gallery owner part of his cash.

Shaken and in utter disbelief, Chris was now sitting in his car, parked in one of the rougher neighborhoods in town, feeling terrible about what he had just done. It made him so sick that he vomited right out the window onto the ground. After a short while, he got out of his car and was immediately approached by three rough-looking men. Chris knew from previous experience that the men were Gangster Greg, Slow Poke, and Shane.

Slow Poke spoke first, dragging his voice. "Whaaaaaat's up, man?"

Chris spoke fast; he wanted to make this transaction quick. "I got the money. I got the money. But I also need another fix." He said, trying not to let the desperation show in his voice.

Shane replied this time, laughing. "Of course you do."

Slow Poke spoke up again. "You waaaaant another f-"

Gangster Greg cut him off. "Man, shut up... you too slow. I'll handle this." He turned to Chris, "How many times you think you gone come down here and disrespect me?"

"But I got all the money this time and some."

Ganger Greg snatched the money out of Chris' hands.

Chris spoke back, even though this time, he knew that the desperation in his voice was showing. "Hold up, man, that's all I got. C'mon... help a brother out!"

Shane piped up. "Help a brother out? This ain't no discount store, fool!"

"Man, you ain't no brother of mine." Gangster Greg said, joining in. "You're a junky! Did you forget about the interest?" he added, swinging a left hook right into Chris' stomach, causing him to fall to the ground.

All the men appeared to be threatening Chris from different angles; he did not know which way to turn. Whatever superpowers he felt not so long ago while defending Vicky at Terrell's club were gone. The kryptonite punches were strong, and Chris was too weak and stressed to fight back.

Slow Poke walked over slowly and kicked Chris while he was down. Gangster Greg proceeded to pull out a gun, and Slow Poke tried to stop him, shouting, "Greg donnnnnnnnn't!" But he was, per his name, "too slow."

Greg ignored him and fired two shots — one hit Chris in the back and the other in his leg.

Shane looked at Chris in disbelief. "Just another Junky!"

"Let's get out of here!" Slow Poke cried out, grabbing the keys.

"Hey, Slow," Greg said, laughing. "I've never seen you move so fast."

All three men piled into Chris' car, revving the engine to an irresponsible accelerated speed, leaving Chris for dead. Chris was barely moving on the ground, but as he lay there, he could hear them spinning off in the car. He was struggling, gasping, and clinging to embrace another minute of life, but he wasn't dead yet. He had the will to live. Vicky had come back into his life, and he didn't want to lose her... not like this.

Gradually, he began to move across the ground, leaving a trail of stained blood on the pavement, having no idea where he was going but knowing he had to get somewhere fast. If he didn't get help soon, he would be found dead with little or no time to repent and plead for his soul. If he could no longer lift his burdens, he felt there would be no hope for his life. So, determined to survive, Chris continued to drag himself as he painfully scraped his body across the rough slab of concrete until he finally found himself on the steps of a church.

Moments before passing out, he saw the steeple light come on.

CHAPTER **THIRTEEN**

Vicky had never been so worried. She had no idea what had happened to Chris — he wouldn't take off with her painting and vanish from the face of the earth, would he? As days passed, the unimaginable began to seep in, as she feared the worst. All she could think was that something terrible had happened to him. Finally, the phone rang, jolting Vicky out of her thoughts.

Quickly answering it, Vicky yelled, "Chris!" into the receiver.

To her surprise, the voice on the other end responded, "No baby, It's your mother."

Vicky let out a long sigh. "Hey, Mom! I'm sorry... I thought you were Chris." She felt the cloud of worry and despair come over her again.

Monica took a deep breath on the other end of the phone. She knew that what she was about to tell her daughter was going to hurt her tremendously. "Baby, that's why I'm calling. I just got off the phone with his mother... Chris has been shot."

Vicky couldn't believe what she was hearing. "Shot! Oh no, when? How? Mom, is he...?" Her voice trembled, her hands shook, and she could barely form a coherent thought, let alone a full sentence.

Monica knew what her daughter was implying and made sure she responded fast, "No, No, he's not dead."

Vicky only allowed herself to feel relief for a brief moment before asking, "Where is he?"

"He's at Memorial Hospital. I can meet you there if you like."

"Okay, Mom. I'm on my way."

Vicky and her mother had arrived at the hospital that evening in a flurry of panic and worry. To her relief, Chris was now awake. He'd had a close call but made it through. However, although happy that his life was no longer in grave danger, this was also a wake-up call; he could not fully enjoy his good fortune and second chance at life in any real way because he was in utter disbelief at what he had done to Vicky. Selling her painting to buy drugs was a new low for him; she was his friend, and she had trusted him with her most prized possession work of art thus far after being fired from her gig. All he could do was sit in a pitiful state at the hospital and reflect on what a terrible thing he had done to her.

Outside Chris' room, Vicky was receiving information about his condition from one of the nurses. "The doctors don't think he will ever walk again, but he will live. He has been awake for a few days, but he's not speaking. He only nods. Vicky, do you think maybe you can get a word out of him?"

Vicky decided to accept this challenge to make Chris speak. She didn't quite know why, but she had a funny feeling that she would be able to get him to talk again. Walking into the room, she sat by his bed, holding his hand as he lay there.

"Can you talk?" Vicky asked in a soft and gentle tone. "Can you explain what happened? Did Terrell do this?" She was trying not to cry, but she couldn't quite help one singular tear escaping as she thought about how worried she had been about him. "Everyone is praying that you are okay. I was so worried about you."

Chris did not respond but instead turned away from her as tears began to flow down his face.

"Are you crying? Are you in pain?" Vicky asked, grabbing his arm.

As she did so, his monitor began to make a loud noise causing the nurse to come in and rush Vicky out while closing the curtains behind them and leaving Vicky standing in the hallway crying and confused.

Several weeks went by, and although Vicky desperately wanted to make Chris speak, she could not. However, as time passed, as Chris slowly healed from his injuries, he knew he had to call Monica and tell her what had happened. He wasn't yet ready to tell Vicky, but he needed advice from someone who knew her best and could help him figure out what to do about the desolate situation.

Taking time to compose himself, Chris gave Monica all the infamous details. He shared how badly he had messed up, coming clean and facing his transgressions. He didn't leave anything out, as painful as it was.

To his surprise, Monica did not shout or yell. She didn't storm out or tell him to leave her daughter alone and get out of their lives for good. Instead, she offered him the best advice he would ever receive in life.

"Chris, sometimes we are guided and misguided in directions we don't always understand. But God willing, he allows us another chance to redeem ourselves. A pathway and a purpose for your life have been carved, but it's up to you to get on the right road and stop following paths that lead you nowhere."

Pausing for a moment, Monica watched for Chris' reaction before continuing. "I overheard one of the doctors say you have a drug problem. Let them help you get into a program; you have so much talent. I don't want to see a young life cut short. Use what God gives you, or he'll find someone more worthy to give it to. The truth is everybody makes mistakes, but you must learn to let the Spirit intercede when you are at your lowest. I just hope you have learned your lesson at this point and will do the right thing, not just for your sake but for hers."

After making sure that Chris was okay, Monica left the room, where she bumped into Vicky, who was shocked to see her there.

"Mom! What are you doing here?"

Monica sighed but looked at Vicky with hopeful eyes. "Baby, we just had to talk. Go on in... he's waiting for you."

Vicky hugged her mother and opened the door to Chris' room. "I just ran into Mom. What's going on?"

Chris knew right then and there, seeing the look of confusion and hurt in Vicky's eyes, was as if he were depriving her of air and that it was time to tell her what he had done and what had driven him to that awful, humiliating place. "Vicky, I have a confession to make. For years I have been struggling to do the right thing. After we graduated, my mother convinced me to attend music school in New York. It took me years to get you out of my head."

Vicky had never been so confused. "What are you talking about?"

Chris took a deep breath. "I have been in love with you since we were little kids, girl."

"In love…?"

"I tried to tell you," Chris continued. "I wrote you, but when you never responded. I lost hope. I lost my soul mate. I felt I had lost everything. But the sound of music kept me alive; it kept me going."

"I never received any letters… Wait a minute! Is that

why my mother was here? Is she on some kind of guilt trip?"

"You know what... I think that's what she was trying to tell me."

"I hope you're not blaming me for something my mother did; she has always tried to protect me."

Chris moved quickly to correct Vicky from the thought process she was on, "No, dear! No! never… Listen, I have something else to tell you… I sold your painting for a quick fix. Whatever I'm going through, it's my fault, not yours. I only have myself to blame."

Vicky could feel that her hands were shaking. "This is just too much… I got to go, Chris… I- I have to get out of here. You should be sorry, and I hope you feel better." The deceit was too much for her to process. But, moving toward the door, Vicky bumped into Chris' hospital bed and hit his leg on purpose, causing Chris to cry out in pain.

"Ouch!"

Vicky did not care. She continued out of his room, almost falling while running down the hospital hallway, trying to find her way out the nearest exit door. Then, something in her peripheral vision caught her eye, making her turn and stop still in her tracks. In the middle of the bland white corridor, she was standing right in front of her beloved painting — Black praying hands with a pyramid standing tall and proud behind them. Perplexed, she knew deep in her soul that God was trying to communicate something to her. What else could it possibly be? "What are you trying to tell me?"

Needing understanding, Vicky returned to Chris' room only to find him sleeping again, but she knew she could not leave this alone until she had some real concrete answers. "Chris, wake up!"

Chris opened his eyes slowly and said, "My God, am I dead? Because an Angel is standing over me!"

Vicky rolled her eyes in frustration. "Stop playing! Angels don't holler… They don't hit either!"

"Then, why are you here?"

"C'mon, get up. I have something to show you."

I can't walk…," Chris objected, looking confused.

"That's right... I forgot, I broke your leg. Let me get you a wheelchair."

Once Vicky had moved Chris into a wheelchair, she began to push him down the hallway she had just come from, viewing her painting.

"You know I'd follow you anywhere," Chris said hesitantly. "But you wouldn't be trying to kill me, would you?"

"Don't tempt me… For once, let me lead the way," Vicky replied. "I think God is trying to tell me something, tell you something… tell us something!"

From a distance, Chris could already see what she was referring to. "Stop! Vicky, please stop! What?! How? My God… My God!"

Vicky had a smile on her face as the two of them stared

at the painting. Her painting. She was simply in awe of the moment.

Moments later, Vicky had marched straight to the reception desk to try and get a better handle on what had happened for her painting to have arrived in the hospital after what Chris had told her. She knew that Chris wasn't lying about what he had done — how could he? He knew it came with the risk of making her hate him forever.

"Hi, excuse me," she said to the receptionist. "Can you get the administrator for me, please?"

The receptionist looked bored. "Sure... may I ask what this is about?"

Vicky upped the urgency in her tone, knowing that it had to count for something in a hospital environment. "Just get me the administrator, please..."

"Okay, give me one second," the receptionist replied, getting up and going to the back office. Seconds later, she returned with the administrator, who approached Vicky.

"Hi, may I help you?"

"Yes, can you tell me how you guys received the painting in the hallway?"

The administrator looked confused. "Which painting? We have several," she asked, looking confused.

Vicky led the administrator down the elongated hallway and back to where her painting was hung against the plain white wall.

"Ah yes... this painting was donated to us."

"Can you tell me who donated it? Vicky asked.

"I can... but why do you ask?"

"It was stolen from me. Wait... it was sold… never mind! I'm the one who painted it, and I would like it back."

"I understand. I'll see what I can do."

"Thank you," Vicky said, staring at the painting a bit longer with tears rolling down her face.

CHAPTER **FOURTEEN**

Three months later, Chris had completed detox and was out of rehab — the beautiful facility outside the city limits allowed him to overcome his struggles, and he received unparalleled care from the exceptionally well-trained staff that helped heal him mentally, physically, and spiritually, giving him a second chance in life.

Following the program, he checked in with Monica, who gave him Andre's number. The day had come when Chris knew he would have to have a man-to-man conversation about Vicky with her father; he needed to clear the air. So, he made the call, and the two men agreed to meet at Andre's house.

It was a modest home with all the furnishings of a bachelor, but the smell of a woman's cheap perfume lingered. Chris scanned the room and noticed a woman's purse, so he got right to the point, informing Andre of his past drug use and recent recovery, as well as the torment that led up to his transgressions from longing for his daughter for years.

"I was simply not able to cope without her," Chris explained. "I felt as if I wasn't even living... I was just existing. Other times I was only floating. "Have you ever felt that way about anyone, Sir?"

Andre sat very quietly for a moment. Although he wasn't the perfect father, Andre had been the one who encouraged Vicky to stay true to her craft over the years, supplying Vicky with a different art kit every year since her ninth birthday. However, he had invariably allowed Monica to take the credit. Still, he grew suspicious of why Chris wanted to talk. "To answer your question, yes... I have been foolish. I couldn't see which way the wind was blowing, even when it hit me in the face. I found myself bargaining with what I was getting for free and compromising my family, not understanding there would be consequences. As men, we don't have to mess up... we choose to mess up."

Chris nodded in agreement and continued to express how he messed up as well but promised "on his life" that he would never hurt Vicky again.

Andre allowed him to confide in him as he patiently listened. "I appreciate you coming here, but this is real talk. If you ever do anything to hurt my daughter," Andre said, leaning closer to Chris, "I will kill you myself. Do I make myself clear? Now go ahead and ask me what you really came over here for."

Vicky was sitting at a dinner table in a beautiful mansion, unable to fully comprehend the twists and turns that had brought her to this moment. Her painting was leaning on a wall in the middle of the dining room while Vicky and Chris sat together. They were having dinner with the Millers, a white couple in their mid-sixties who had only recently come into their lives; they were the ones who had donated Vicky's painting to the hospital.

"Thank you, Mr. and Mrs. Miller, for having us over for dinner," said Vicky politely.

"Please, call me John."

"And me, Sarah."

John looked at the painting and then over at Vicky. "My wife was very moved by this painting you created, and she said I just had to see it."

"Oh, really?" Vicky said, surprised.

"Yes. But I decided we wouldn't keep it because of the color of the hands. But we did want to donate it; that's how it ended up at the hospital. We felt that someone would be able to benefit from its presence.

"John!" Sarah scolded.

"I'm sorry, I have to be honest," he replied.

"No, that's okay. Feel free to speak your mind, John," Vicky said softly.

"Well, I assume those praying hands are of Jesus, correct?" asked Mr. Miller.

Vicky remained confident in her responses. "Yes, they are."

"I thought so. How do you know Jesus was that color?" Mr. Miller replied matter of factly.

Chris joined in the conversation. "Well, Sir... everyone is entitled to their opinion."

"Chris!" Vicky shouted.

"It's okay. I'm just saying, what is your source? Any reason you painted him... Black?" Mr. Miller continued.

Vicky took a breath before speaking again. Normally, this type of confrontation would make her uncomfortable and nervous, but she believed in her art and what it stood for wholeheartedly; nothing was going to change her mind. "Sure, there actually is a reason for that. In my opinion, it's not about skin color... Michelangelo painted him with blue eyes, so as an artist, I view him as a person of my skin color. Is anything wrong with that?"

Mr. Miller laughed heartily.

"You can laugh all you want to, Sir. It's true for me. You see, Jesus went by many names: Son of God, Matthew 2:15. Prince of Peace, Isaiah 9:6. Heru or Horus carved in stones In Egypt. First Begotten, Revelation 1:5. King of Kings, First Timothy 6:15. The Great High Priest, also the Son of God. I have to reemphasize Hebrews 4:14, The Lion of the Tribe of Judah, Revelation 5:5... and where is Judea located? In Israel, which used to be Canaan, which is in Africa. You might have to look at an older map; however, do the research yourself. How familiar are you with the Bible, John?"

"I've read it before, but it's been a long time," said Mr. Miller.

"Well, let me refresh your memory. If you remember correctly, Jesus went to Egypt. Let's turn to Matthew 2 verse 14, hence why the pyramid is in the background of the painting."

They both turned to look at Vicky's praying hands painting.

"Also, Jesus is from Jerusalem, in Israel, which is in Africa. However, today, it is considered the Middle East; that's what history teaches us... doesn't it? Also, his hair was nappy like wool, and his feet were the color of bronze."

Mr. and Mrs. Miller looked dumbfounded. Clearly, this was not a conversation they ever expected to have, especially with someone as young as Vicky.

"What? You don't believe me?" Vicky continued. "Look it up. Revelations chapter 1, verses 14 and 15. Go ahead. Where are your cell phones at? Depending on what version you're reading from, for some reason, it has been removed... and I question why?" Vicky said with conviction and passion.

The older couple remained speechless.

However, Chris wasn't satisfied leaving the total weight of the discussion on the woman he loved, so he dove in. "Have you heard of the Council of Nicaea 325 AD? Also, for the record, one the oldest churches on planet earth carved out of stone is located in Ethiopia... the church of Lalibela, you may know them as the Kushites,

2nd Kings 19, verse 9. However, when you offend my queen, that insults me."

Motioning for Vicky to stand, Chris said, "Thank you, Sir... peace and blessings to you," as the pair walked out of the mansion.

Once they had made it outside, he continued, laughing, "WOW! It upsets me when people act like we don't know our history! For example, Garrett Morgan, who invented the three-signal traffic light... a Black man. Damm... Just imagine how the world would be without it."

"Yeah, one big traffic jam," Vicky stated.

Both now chuckling about the exchange that had just happened, before carefully placing the canvas bearing the praying hands with the pyramid face up, so as not to damage it, they put it directly behind them into the back of the vehicle where the seat was already let down.

"You sure told them," Vicki said, driving away from the mansion.

"Just had to do a little teaching, that's all," Chris said proudly from the passenger seat. "Speaking of... somebody has been reading their Bible!" replied Chris.

Vicky smiled. "You don't think I went to church with my mother all those years and didn't learn a little something, do you?"

As they drove back toward Vicky's home, she found that she was turned on by the way he had stood by her side. He had evolved into a fully grown man — physically and mentally. No, I'm not doing this to myself again, she thought to herself. Finally, Vicky knew that it was time to have the conversation with him at long last. "You know what, Chris? If I didn't know you better, I would think you would be friends with the devil. Why on earth would you sell a painting that had been revealed to me by God himself?"

Chris sighed. He, too, had known that this was inevitable. "Vicky, I was on drugs. Drugs are from the devil. They make you do things that you are not even aware of that you are doing. It's like you are possessed and have no control over your mind and body. So, in a way, I guess you're right... I WAS friends with the devil. But not anymore."

Vicky took a long pause, keeping her eyes on the road. She exhaled long and slow before responding. "I forgive you. "

"Look, Vicky... I want to talk to you about something."

"What the hell you want? Forgive me, Father God," Vicky exclaimed, looking upwards.

"Damn, girl. Attitude?"

"I'm still a little pissed off that you sold the painting! It is priceless."

"I said I was sorry and wasn't myself when I did that. Plus, you just told me that you forgive me."

Vicky sighed again, realizing that she hadn't been entirely honest when she said that. The truth was that she wanted to forgive Chris, but what he had done was terrible

— whether he had been on drugs at the time or not. "Half of me does. The other half doesn't. Give the other half some time, though... she'll come around."

"Ummm, okay," Chris replied.

"Now, what do you want to talk to me about?"

"Vicky, we've known each other since we were kids, and I have never felt like this with any other woman in my entire life," Chris said, slowly reaching into his pocket. Pulling out a small diamond ring, he asked, "So, with that being said, will you marry me?"

Vicky glanced over at him, shocked. "What's that in your hand? Is that a bubble gum ring?"

"C'mon, Babe... don't spoil the moment," Chris said with sweet intensity. "I was going to ask you later this evening, but I couldn't wait any longer."

Vicky pulled the car over to the side of the road and parked it before looking over at Chris, her face deadly serious. "What did you just ask me? "Aren't you supposed to get down on one knee or something?"

"I asked if you would marry me, sweetheart. Now you know if I get down on one knee, you're going to have to help me back up with this cane.

CHAPTER
FIFTEEN

"Vicky, are you okay? What's wrong?" Chris asked, immediately concerned by her silence.

"After everything we've been through..." she paused again. "I realize how much I love you. So yes, of course... I will marry you!"

"Yes! Alright, cool!"

For the first time, they had both been as truthful to one another as they could be, kissing and embracing as if there were no tomorrow to worry about.

"I do have one question," Vicky said, breaking off the kiss.

"What's that?" He smiled.

"How is your broke behind gonna pay for our wedding?"

They both laughed at that.

"Well, it just so happens that I have a wealthy uncle."

"Chris! If we're gonna get married, we have to be totally honest with each other."

"What? You don't believe me?" Chris replied, pulling out his cell phone and scrolling through his contacts. Once he found the entry he was looking for, he turned the device toward Vicky.

UNCLE TOM (717) 555-2222

Vicky burst out laughing at the name on the phone screen, "Your uncle's name is Tom?"

"Yeah. What's wrong with that?" Chris asked, innocently serious.

"Uncle Tom? For real?" Vicky could not contain her laughter.

"Oh, you got jokes. Actually, his name is Timothy, but we call him Tom as his joke name. Since this is a serious situation, I'm going to call him by his real name. He told me to let him know if I ever needed anything."

"Oh, okay, I was about to say..."

"Give me a second," Chris replied, dialing his Uncle Tim. After three rings, Vicky could hear a muffled voice on the other end of the phone.

"Hello?"

"Hey, Uncle Tim... it's Chris."

"Chris! Long time no talk nor see. How are you, nephew?"

"I'm alright. How are you doing?"

"Oh, just hanging out like usual. Chantelle let me know

that you are doing so much better since you were in the hospital. You had us all worried there for a minute. What's been going on since then? How's the music thing been going?"

"It's going alright. I'm working on it, Uncle Tim, I'm working on it."

"That's good. Keep at it. Work hard. Remember that no one is going to hand you an opportunity. You have to create one for yourself."

"I know, Unc. I know."

"So, what's going on?"

"Remember you said if I ever needed anything to let you know?"

"Yeah, yeah, uh huh. Why? What's up?"

"I'm gonna need that favor right about now," Chris said.

"I thought paying for all those doctor bills was enough," Tim replied with a chuckle.

"Oh! Mom said it was taken care of... I'm sorry, Uncle Tim. I should have known it was you. Okay then, one more favor."

"Alright then. What are you talkin', nephew? Speak to me."

"Well, I want to get married, and I was hoping you could pay for the wedding."

"Oh really? Wow, nephew! Congratulations! Who's the lucky lady?"

"Her name is Vicky. We've been knowing each other ever since we were kids," Chris shared.

"Why, of course... I remember her. Childhood sweethearts... that's cool. But marriage is a big step, Chris. Are you sure you are ready for that?"

Chris glanced over at Vicky, looking intently at him from the driver's seat, and said, "I haven't been more sure about anything else in my entire life."

Vicky teared up again and forced a smile across her face. These were happy tears. Even after all that Chris had put her through, she was absolutely, positively sure about this.

"Alright, nephew... I will be honored to help you out with your wedding. But I only ask you for one thing."

"What's that?"

"Don't go too crazy now. After the pandemic, I've been on a budget." "Okay, Uncle Tim. I got you."

Uncle Tim laughed and resumed a light tone. "I'm just kidding, nephew. You only get married once. Go all out."

"Thanks, Unc," Chris said as he and Vicky smiled at each other.

"Alright, send me the details. Talk to you soon."

Chris hung up and looked at Vicky, who stared back at him. At first, Chris thought she was just excited about the wedding planning being confirmed, but when he looked a little closer, he could see something else was on her mind. "What? What's wrong? Why are you looking at me like that?" he asked.

"Do you remember that night?" she replied, still watching him intently. "What night?"

Vicky cleared her throat. "You know... that night," she said, more slowly and clearly.

"Huh?" Chris said, still confused. "What are you talking about?"

"You really don't remember?"

"Remember what?" Chris asked, ready to get to the bottom of this back and forth. "What are you talking about?"

"I can't believe you don't remember. That's just like a man!

"Whoa, whoa, whoa... what are you tripping off of, Vicky? What night?"

Vicky did not say a word but looked at Chris with an angry expression on her face.

Chris thought for a second, thinking of all of the different things she could be referring to before it clicked, and he finally remembered what Vicky was speaking about.

"Ohhhhhh, that night. When we…"

"Yes!" Vicky was nearly shouting now but laughing at the same time. She loved this man, but he could be frustrating at times!

"Yeah, what about it? Wait… You're not-"

Before Chris could finish, Vicky took a big breath and shouted, "Yes… I'm pregnant!"

"What? For real?" Chris looked shocked, excited, and ecstatic all at the same time.

"Yes! So your timing is perfect because I wasn't trying to have a baby out of wedlock."

Chris took her by the hand, "It's actually God's timing too."

"You got that right. Are you sure you're ready for all of this? You're gonna have to be both a husband and a father. You have a family now."

"Girl, I know."

"I'm just saying, Chris... you're gonna have to be a provider. I'll need help with car notes, bills and doctor's appointments, changing diapers, etc. We are not depending on your Uncle Tom… I mean, Uncle Tim. Whoever he is… he is not the father."

"I know. I have my associate's degree in music. I can probably get a job with benefits as a teacher..."

"Well, you need your bachelor's degree for something like that, but maybe you can try getting a teaching job at a community college or elementary school."

"Yeah, that might work."

"Either way, Chris, I believe in you."

"Thanks, babe, that means a lot. You know, we're in our mid-twenties, and I don't see myself being with any other woman but you. "Chris said sincerely.

"That's so sweet, but remember, actions speak louder than words." This she meant with all of her heart. Chris would have to prove himself to her, not just make promises. She had relied on words all too often and had learned the hard way that, more often than not, they were not enough.

"I understand that," Chris said, interrupting her thought. "So what's it going to be?"

"No, I don't want to know ahead of time; I want it to be a beautiful surprise. God has blessed us thus far. Besides, it's out of our hands. But the doctors said everything looked fine.

"Alright, cool'. Hey, let's go to the beach and celebrate!"

"Right now?"

"Yes, right now! Why not?"

"Dang boy, sometimes you can be romantic, but other times, you can also be a jerk."

"Dang, lay off me, Vicky. Give a brotha a break!"

They laughed together at that, and Vicky put the car back into gear and started driving in the direction of the coastline.

That evening, Vicky and Chris walked along the shore, holding hands. At regular intervals, they stopped, faced each other, then kissed, with waves crashing in the background and the moonlight shining over them.

Over the weeks to come, the couple spent their days planning their wedding. They checked out wedding venues and sampled seemingly infinite pieces of wedding cakes, and Vicky tried on dresses until she found the perfect one, with Chris doing the same thing in tuxedos.

When the time came for their wedding day, they held it in Uncle Tim's backyard, a small and beautiful reception with a variety of food spread across the different tables and a small crowd gathered around.

As Chris and Vicky stood at the altar, saying their vows with Reverend Hopkins marrying them, no one seemed to notice the slight baby bump. Deep down, they knew they wanted to please God and do the right thing together. They both said "I do" with love and tears of joy in their eyes and hearts, and just like that, it was official... they were married.

The crowd cheered and clapped as Vicky and Chris embraced in a long-awaited first kiss as husband and wife, and all the pain and passion had ultimately survived through *Love and Art.*

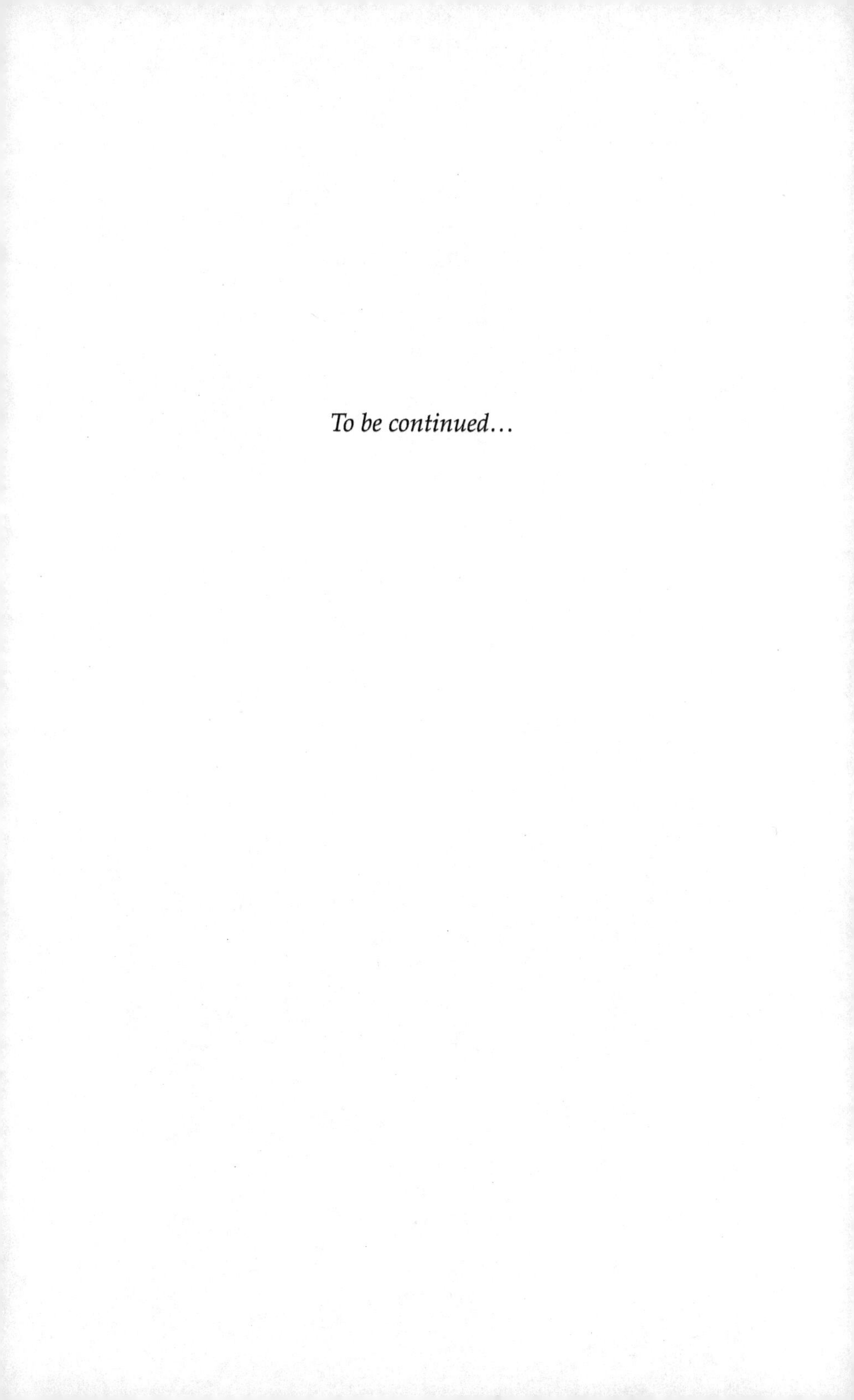

To be continued…

www.ingramcontent.com/pod-product-compliance
Lightning Source LLC
La Vergne TN
LVHW090614110826
845146LV00001B/382